Sweden

Sweden

BY SYLVIA MCNAIR

Enchantment of the World
Second Series

Children's Press®

A Division of Grolier Publishing

NEW YORK   LONDON   HONG KONG   SYDNEY
DANBURY, CONNECTICUT

This book is dedicated to the memory of two special friends
who encouraged and inspired me to start writing books:
the late Franklin Folsom and the late Chandler Forman.

Visit the Children's Press® web site at http://publishing.grolier.com

Consultant: Börje Vähämäki, Professor of Finnish Studies, University of Toronto

Please note: *All statistics are as up-to-date as possible at the time of publication.*

Library of Congress Cataloging-in-Publication Data

McNair, Sylvia.
      Sweden / by Sylvia McNair.
      p. cm. — (Enchantment of the world. Second series)
      Includes bibliographical references and index.
Summary: Describes the history, geography, economy, culture, religion, language,
      sports, arts, and people of this Northern European country.
      ISBN 0-516-20607-9
      1. Sweden—Juvenile literature. [1. Sweden.] I. Title. II. Series
      DL609.M36 1998
      948.5—dc21   97-26886
                                    CIP
                                    AC

Acknowledgments

The author gratefully acknowledges the assistance and encouragement of the staff of the Swedish-American Museum of Chicago and the Swedish Information Service, New York. Thanks also to Charles Peterson of North Park College, Stina Hirsch, and, as always, Anna Lokensgard Idol.

Contents

Cover photo:
Midsummer festival

The beautiful Swedish countryside

The royal family

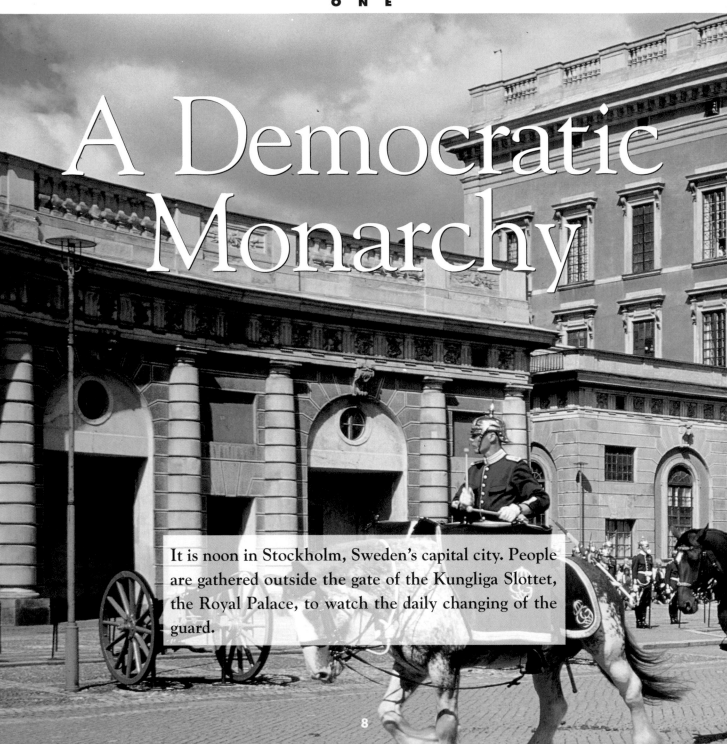

A Democratic Monarchy

It is noon in Stockholm, Sweden's capital city. People are gathered outside the gate of the Kungliga Slottet, the Royal Palace, to watch the daily changing of the guard.

MEMBERS OF THE ROYAL GUARD IN FULL-DRESS UNIFORM, with white boots, gloves, and hats, march across the bridge that connects two of Stockholm's islands. Two sentries stand at the main gate, ignoring the cameras flashing all around them. Two flag bearers head the procession. The national flag, a yellow cross on a blue field, is flanked by another bearing the Swedish Great Seal. Drums roll, and the military band plays stirring martial music to accompany the ceremony.

A view of the Royal Palace from Stockholm's harbor

In the palace yard are several cannons on wheels. The soldiers about to be relieved stand at the ready, their guns topped with bayonets.

The ritual takes place in front of the largest royal residence in the world. The symbol of the monarchy, it is used for important state ceremonies and for royal offices, but the present royal family no longer lives there. The crown jewels are kept

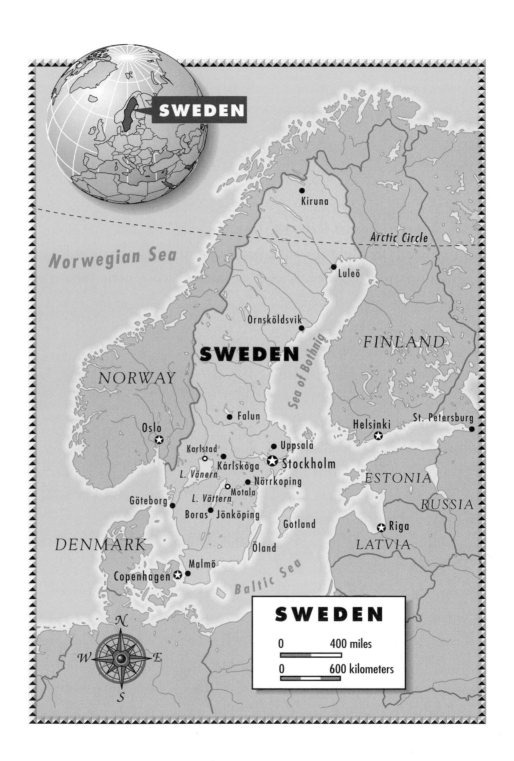

Geographical map
of Sweden

in vaults beneath the palace. Some of the building's 608 rooms are open for public tours.

King Carl and Queen Silvia preside over public ceremonies and are the formal representatives of the nation. They mix with the citizens at concerts, theatrical productions, and sports events. They are royalty with a common touch. The king has said he believes his royal duty is to be a moral leader, not a political one.

Both visitors and citizens like to watch the changing of the guard. They enjoy the pomp and pageantry that symbolize Sweden's many centuries as a monarchy. Yet this nation is actually one of the most democratic in the world. And despite the military uniforms, music, and weaponry, Sweden is a country dedicated to neutrality and peace.

King Carl and Queen Silvia bring elegance to every event.

Land and Water

Water, water, everywhere. About half of Sweden's boundaries are on the water—the Baltic Sea on the east and the North Sea on the southwest. The coastline is 4,720 miles (7,600 km) long. No wonder the Swedish people have such a long history as seafarers.

THERE'S A LOT OF WATER INLAND, TOO. THERE ARE BETWEEN 90,000 and 100,000 lakes, depending on who is counting. In addition, there are more than 20,600 miles (34,333 km) of rivers. Most of the rivers are not usable for transportation, but they are a valuable natural resource. They furnish hydroelectric power for Sweden's cities and industries.

Sweden is a long, narrow country. It is three times as long from north to south (977 miles or 1,572 km) as it is from east to west (310 miles or 499 km). With an area of 173,732 square

A flood of water from a Swedish hydroelectric plant

miles (449,964 sq km), it is the fifth-largest European nation. Only Russia, Ukraine, France, and Spain are larger.

North of the Baltic Sea, a short part of the eastern boundary is shared with Finland, and Norway is the next-door neighbor on the west. The Baltic Straits separate Sweden from Denmark.

What Is Scandinavia?

Thousands of years ago, glaciers covered all of northern Europe. As they melted, they left behind a huge lake over much of

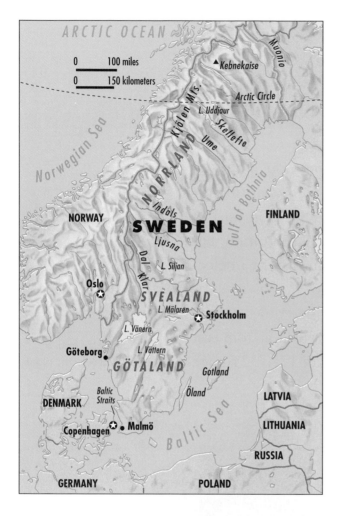

the northern land. The waters drained off into the seas, and the land began to rise. The flow of the waters separated the Scandinavian Peninsula from the rest of Europe. A ridge of mountains was left, stretching north to south along the middle of the peninsula.

Sweden and Norway make up the Scandinavian Peninsula. Denmark was once connected to that land. Its shape shows that it could fit right into the space between the southern tips of the other two countries.

Today there are five Nordic, or Scandinavian, countries. The other two are Iceland and Finland. The five are connected through a shared history, similar languages (except for Finland), and a desire to cooperate with one another for their common good.

Topograpical map of Sweden

Sweden and Norway make up the Scandinavian Peninsula.

Götaland

Southern Sweden, Götaland, has two types of terrain, the lowlands and the highlands. Skåne (Scania), has forests and fertile valleys and plains. It is the best agricultural region of Sweden. The land is similar to the area in Denmark and northern Germany that was once connected to it. The coastal cities of Skåne were important trading ports during the Middle Ages. Some of the traders grew very rich and built mansions in the region. More than 200 castles and huge homes remain.

Småland, just north of Skåne, has an irregular rocky coastline on the Baltic Sea. There are many bays and inlets, white cliffs, and sandy beaches. Rough, low islands lie offshore. One of them, Öland, is 85 miles (137 km) long.

Skåne has fertile valleys and plains.

A lighthouse on the island of Öland

A Look at Sweden's Cities

Göteborg (shown above) is Scandinavia's largest port and the tenth largest in Europe. It is Sweden's second largest city. Göteborg grew out of a Viking settlement in the eleventh century, and in 1621 King Gustav II Adolph granted Göteborg a charter to establish a free trade port. The city is located on both banks of the Göta River. Several industries are important to Göteborg, including Volvo, the world famous automobile manufacturer. In 1995, Göteborg had an estimated population of 444,553.

Malmö is the capital of the province of Skåne and Sweden's third largest city. The name Malmö means sand mounds. Until 1658, Malmö was under Danish rule. Its industries include textile manufacturing, food processing, and shipbuilding. Its population was estimated to be about 242,706 in 1995.

Uppsala is Sweden's principal university town. Viking ceremonies continued to be followed into the eleventh century, well after the introduction of Christianity into Sweden. Uppsala University was founded in 1477 by Archbishop Jakob Ulfson. The university remained the chief function of Uppsala for centuries. Uppsala lies along both banks of the Fyris River. It had an estimated population of about 181,191 in 1995.

For more information on Sweden's capital and largest city, Stockholm, see Chapter Six.

Glasswork factories in Småland are famous for their fine products. On the west coast is Göteborg (Gothenburg), one of Sweden's three largest cities. The other two are Malmö, in Skåne, and Stockholm, the capital of Sweden. Göteborg is a port city, with the largest harbor in Sweden.

The southern uplands have poorer soils and a cooler, wetter climate than the lowlands. Hills in the north slope steeply down to plains. There are patches of peat bogs and clay deposits. Two-thirds of the land is in forest, with a rich mixture of deciduous (leafy) and coniferous (cone-bearing) trees.

From an airplane one can see a very neat and regular checkerboard pattern to the towns and farms of southern Sweden. That is because the kings of Sweden encouraged careful town planning during the seventeenth and eighteenth centuries.

The plains of Svealand

A seventeenth-century wall still stands in Visby.

Svealand

North of the southern highlands is Svealand. The name means "land of the Swedes." Svealand has rolling hills, lakes, and plains. The land slopes eastward from a plateau in the west to a narrow coastal plain along the Baltic Sea.

A mild and wet climate gives west central Sweden a long growing season. Agriculture and fishing are important industries.

The large island of Gotland, northeast of Öland, is part of central Sweden. Visby, a town on the island, dates from the Middle Ages. (The Middle Ages cover the period from about A.D. 500 to 1500.) More than 150 original structures still exist, some of them very well preserved. Gotland's natural beauty includes unusual limestone rock formations and a great many wildflowers.

Stockholm, Sweden's capital and largest city, is near the eastern coast of Svealand. Stockholm has been called the Venice of the North, because there is water everywhere. The city is built on fourteen islands that lie between Lake Mälaren and the Baltic Sea. Nearby is an archipelago of 24,000 islands. These islands are often called Stockholm's pearl necklace.

Wildflowers and limestone add to the beauty of Gotland's countryside.

Stockholm is a beautiful and cosmopolitan city with amazingly clean streets. (Littering isn't common in Sweden.) The city and its five neighboring provinces make up the most populated region of the country. A large number of suburbs surround the city. In summer, many residents leave the city for their vacation cottages on peninsulas and islands.

Stockholm is a city built on islands.

Sweden's Geographical Features

Location: 55 degrees 20' to 69 degrees 4' N; 10 degrees 58' to 24 degrees 10' E

Area: 173,732 square miles (449,964 sq km)

Highest Elevation: Mt. Kebnekaise 6,926 feet (2,111 m)

Lowest Elevation: Sea level along the coast

Coastline: 4,700 miles (7,600 km)

Annual Average Rainfall: In Stockholm, 22 inches (55 cm); in Göteborg, 26 inches (67 cm)

Largest Lake: Lake Vänern 2,156 square miles (5,584 sq km), 91 miles (146 km) long, and 328 feet (100 m) deep

Major Rivers: the Göta, the Dal, the Angerman, the Ume, and the Luleålv

Largest City: Stockholm est. population of 703,627 (1995)

Average Temperatures in Stockholm: February, 22° to 30°F (−5° to −1°C); July, 57° to 70°F (14° to 21°C)

Neighbors and Boundary Lengths: Norway to the west, 1,006 miles (1,619 km); Denmark to the south (across Kattegat); Finland to the east, 364 miles (586 km); Gotland Island coastline, 249 miles (400 km); Öland Island coastline, 45 miles (72 km)

Territorial Sea Limit: 12 miles (20 km)

There are several large lakes in central Sweden. North of lakes Hjälmaren and Mälaren are fertile plains. Going northwest, the land changes to forested hills and valleys, then to mountains at the Norwegian border.

Lake Mälaren

Dalarna, in north central Sweden, is known as the Folklore District. Summertime is celebrated with many festivals. Villagers dress in traditional costumes, perform folk dances, and provide open-air entertainment. Farms and meadows cover much of the southeastern corner of Dalarna.

Dalarna hosts many summertime festivals.

A copper mine at Falun

The red paint on this summer cottage contains Falun copper, which protects the house from severe weather.

Copper was dug in the city of Falun for more than a thousand years. At its peak, this mine produced two-thirds of the world's copper. Zinc and iron have also been mined here. Today, tourists come to Falun to take tours of the mine, which is no longer in commercial production.

Many summer cottages in Sweden are painted red. The paint contains Falun copper, which provides an excellent protection from harsh weather. This paint is also used on ships, yachts, boats, and oil storage depots.

Much of the land is covered in forest. The mountains of northern Dalarna overlook a high plateau with extensive peat deposits. The landscape also includes broad open valleys, long lakes, historic farm buildings, and industrial relics.

Norrland

Norrland, northern Sweden, occupies three-fifths of the nation's land. There are vast stretches of wilderness where no one lives. The far north is above the Arctic Circle (*Polcirkeln*). In Arctic lands, the sun never sets completely in summer months, and it can't be seen at all during most of the winter. Arctic regions are nicknamed "lands of the Midnight Sun."

Sweden's far north is also known as Lapland. Lapland has no distinct boundaries, and Lapland is not a nation. It is the land where people called Sami, formerly called Lapps, have lived since prehistoric times. It covers an area stretching from Norway across Sweden and Finland into Russia.

The "land of the Midnight Sun"

A Sami girl

Primary Land Use and Resources

Cereals, dairy	**Ag**	Silver
Dairy, general farming	**Au**	Gold
Light farming	**Cu**	Copper
Forests	**Fe**	Iron ore
Sheep herding	**Pb**	Lead
Nonagricultural	**U**	Uranium
Industrial	**Zn**	Zinc
◇ Hydroelectric		

Hiking is very popular.

In the west, along the border with Norway, is the Scandinavian mountain range, the Kjølen. Some of the mountains are topped with small glaciers. The highest peaks of the range are in Norway. The highest peak in Sweden is called Mt. Kebnekaise and is 6,926 feet (2,111 m) above sea level.

Swedish people and tourists from other countries like to hike, hunt, fish, ski, and climb mountains in Norrland.

Winds from the southwest blow over the North Sea and the mountain range, often dumping heavy rainfalls on Sweden.

Swift rivers flowing from the mountains cut broad, deep valleys on their way to the Baltic Sea. Along their journey, they tumble over granite rocks in rapids

Sweden's National Parks

In 1909, Sweden established the first national parks in Europe. Today there are twenty of them, ranging from tiny recreational areas in the south to vast wilderness tracts in the northern mountains. Some of them are sites of legends about trolls and giants. Blå Jungfrun, on an island off of Öland, consists largely of lichen-covered rock formations (center right).

All but four of the parks are in Norrland. Sånfjället, in the province of Härjedalen, is a deep forest largely inhabited by bears.

Six national parks are above the Arctic Circle, in Lapland. Muddus has deep gorges, a lake, and many species of birds and animals. Sareks (above) is an enormous rugged wilderness with mountains, deep valleys, and many glaciers. It is home to bears (right), lynx, arctic foxes, and many other species.

Much of Padjelanta is above the tim-berline, where no trees can grow because the climate is too harsh. One of the oldest and most popular national parks is Abisko. It is a river valley of 30 square miles (77 sq km). The land is covered with birch trees, mosses, and brilliant wildflowers in summer and glows with golden colors in the autumn.

and waterfalls. Occasionally they broaden out to form long, narrow lakes.

East of the mountains is a band of rolling hills. Forests of pine, spruce, and birch are interrupted here and there by wetlands and peat bogs. The slopes are lower and gentler toward the eastern border with Finland. The flatlands are swampy in summer, providing an excellent breeding ground for mosquitoes. Much of this region is barren and nearly empty of people.

South of the Finnish border, Norrland fronts on the Gulf of Bothnia, part of the Baltic Sea. The coastline, just as it is farther south, is very irregular. Hundreds of bays, coves, and inlets are dotted with islands.

Forests cover more than half of Norrland. Almost all the rest of the area is uncultivated mountains and bogs.

The summer is sunny and warm.

Opposite: **Forests and wetlands are prevalent in Sweden.**

Snow and ice cover the ground in winter.

Climate

Even though Sweden is one of the most northerly nations in the world, the climate is not as harsh and cold as you might think. At least not in southern and central Sweden, where most of the people live. From May to August, the weather is usually calm and sunny. Days are long, and temperature levels are almost ideal. The average is around 68°F (20°C), sometimes rising to as warm as 86°F (30°C).

The hours of sunlight begin to shrink in September,

Icebreakers keep the ports open for shipping.

and the leaves turn to lovely autumn shades. Frost may begin in October and snow falls in November. For most of the winter, the ground will be covered with snow, and the temperatures will stay below freezing. Sometimes there are really cold snaps, but these don't come often.

In winter, ice covers most of the lakes and shallow portions of the Baltic Sea. Huge icebreakers are used to keep some of the ports open for shipping. Auto routes are marked over solidly frozen lakes when it is safe to drive on them.

Snow begins to disappear in April. Spring arrives in a rush in May, bringing lots of flowers.

In northern Sweden, the summer begins later and ends earlier than in the south. But the long sunlit days are mild and pleasant in the Arctic. Then comes the season when it is dark and cold for twenty-four hours every day.

In Skåne, the growing season may be eight months long, while in Lapland it is normally only about three months. However, the north has sunshine nearly all the time during those three months. Here, near the North Pole, the sun does not drop below the horizon in summer. This helps crops to grow very large very quickly.

Native Plants and Creatures

Norra Kvills is a tiny national park in Småland. Trees have never been cut in this wild and lush reserve. Some of them are gigantic and very old—hundreds of years old. Many are covered with mosses and lichens. Up north, along the Norwegian border, are mountaintops where no trees grow at all.

A birch forest in autumn

IN BETWEEN THESE TWO EXTREMES, there are many kinds of trees and other plants. At one time, Sweden's southern and southwestern coasts were covered with forests of beech and oak trees. Today neat farmlands have taken the place of many of the forests.

More than half of Sweden is covered by forests. Deciduous trees (those whose leaves shed seasonally), such as beech, oak, ash, elm, maple, and linden trees flourish in the south of Sweden. Toward the north, these hardwoods (another name for deciduous trees) gradually give way to different forest mixtures. Birches, aspens, and mountain ash trees are found among pines and other coniferous (cone-bearing) trees.

In summertime, Swedish families like to hike in the woods and pick berries and mushrooms. They find lingonberries, cloudberries, raspberries, wild strawberries, and blueberries, and they bring these treats home. The berries are eaten with cream or are used in making jams, jellies, juices, and desserts.

Picking mushrooms in
Sweden's woods

Both adults and children can attend classes to learn about the many kinds of mushrooms and to decide which ones are safe to eat.

When spring arrives each year, wildflowers rapidly burst into bloom. Many kinds of wild orchids can be found in different parts of the country. Thirty-five varieties have been counted on the island of Gotland.

Rockroses, anemones, water lilies, lilies of the valley, daisies, and buttercups are some of the blossoms that bring color to the countryside in spring and summer. Everyman's Right does not apply to the picking of wildflowers. Laws protecting rare plants have existed in Sweden for nearly a hundred years.

Everyman's Right

In Sweden, all people are allowed to go freely into forests and help themselves to edible plants. This is an old tradition known as Everyman's Right (Allemansrätt). There are no laws against trespassing on private or public lands. Woods, fields, and beaches are open to everyone. Anyone can hike, go swimming, or tie up a boat anywhere without special permits.

Along with this right, people understand they have a responsibility not to do anything to harm the environment, such as overpicking or littering. And as a matter of courtesy, Swedish people do not walk through other people's gardens or planted fields.

This yellow lady's slipper is among the many types of orchids that bloom in the spring.

Swedish people love flowers and the outdoors. The long, dark days of winter make them especially delighted with the coming of spring and summer. The summer air is filled with the scent of flowers everywhere—inside homes, in yards, in front of public buildings.

Carolus Linnaeus

A Swedish natural scientist named Carolus Linnaeus lived in the eighteenth century. Everyone who has studied botany or biology since that time has felt his influence. He was the first to establish classification systems for plants and animals. He published books that assigned names and identified classes to all plants and animals known at the time. His system has been followed for all new species discovered since then.

Linnaeus was the first person to use the name *Homo sapiens* for humans.

Flowers adorn most homes and public buildings.

A roe deer

Reindeer make their home in Lapland.

Mammals

Even though so much of Sweden is forest, which should be a good habitat for animals, a few of the native mammals have become quite rare. Wolves used to be common in northern Sweden; now they are almost extinct. Strict laws have been passed to protect the bear, wolverine, arctic fox, and lynx. The musk ox, introduced into Sweden from Norway, is also protected, as are whales and otters.

Moose and roe deer are very common. The moose, called an elk in Europe, is actually a traffic hazard. Smaller animals—hares, rabbits, badgers, hedgehogs, ermines, and red squirrels—thrive in the forests.

Reindeer have inhabited the far north—Lapland—for thousands of years. Over time, the Sami (formerly known as Lapps) domesticated herds of reindeer. The reindeer is an all-purpose animal. It is used as a work animal, to haul sleds; its hide is a material for clothing; and reindeer meat is a valuable source of protein.

Lemmings

A tiny animal native to the northern highlands of Sweden and other far north regions is the arctic lemming. A furry animal that looks something like a hamster, it is only 3 to 5 inches (8 to 13 cm) long. Its fur, normally brown, turns white in winter.

Every few years, lemmings migrate in large numbers, in search of new homes. They travel across land and swim across streams and rivers. Sometimes they try to swim over a body of water that is too large, and many of them drown.

Legends have made people believe that lemmings deliberately choose to go on a death march to the sea. Scientists don't believe this theory today. They say the little creatures are just looking for a place that has more food than where they have been living.

Birds

Coastal regions of Sweden attract many thousands of migratory birds. The country's long shoreline and thousands of lakes provide a good habitat for waterfowl. There are several kinds of colorful ducks—teal, blue, eider, and others. They share the watery regions with gulls, terns, snipes, wagtail, and sea eagles.

Ptarmigans and golden plovers like northern climates. Cranes, grouse, and partridge also make their home in Sweden.

The great grey owl is one of Sweden's many species of birds.

Birdwatchers visit Dalby Söderskog National Park in spring when songbirds are there in great numbers. Another favorite park for watching and listening to birds is Stora Mosse. Whooper swans, marsh harriers, and cranes are among the species in this large, flat region.

Fish

The salty Atlantic waters on the west, the less salty Baltic Sea to the east, and the freshwater lakes and rivers in Sweden's interior provide homes for a huge variety of fish and shellfish. No wonder one sees some kind of seafood in most traditional Scandinavian meals.

Swedish fishers find cod, mackerel, herring, and flatfish in the North Sea. Salmon, trout, pike, and perch are caught in lakes and rivers. Large quantities of strömming (Baltic herring) live in the Baltic Sea.

Fishing is a way of life.

Provincial Symbols

Nature is very important to Swedes, and each province has its own symbols from the plant and animal kingdoms. However, Sweden has no symbolic national animal or plant.

Opposite: **Caspian tern**

Who Are the Swedes?

Most of the people in Sweden share a common ancestry. Their forebears were Germanic people who migrated to Scandinavia from lands beyond the Baltic Sea. Early tribes were the Goths, of Götaland, and the Svear, who lived farther north in Svealand.

STILL FARTHER NORTH WERE THE Sami, a native and nomadic people who lived in the Arctic and the sub-arctic regions before the other tribes moved into the southern parts of the Scandinavian peninsula.

Sweden has nearly nine million people. This is the largest population of any of the five Scandinavian countries. Like other Scandinavians, the majority of Swedes are fair-skinned, with light hair and eyes. But this does not apply to everyone. Swedes with dark hair and eyes are not unusual.

The Sami have lived in Sweden for hundreds of years.

Many Swedes have fair skin and blond hair.

Who Are the Swedes? **39**

Runes

Inscriptions written in an ancient alphabet have been found on ancient stones and other hard substances. The inscriptions are called runes, and the alphabet is the runic alphabet. Some four thousand runes have been discovered in northern Europe, Britain, and Iceland. Twenty-five hundred of them are in Sweden.

The oldest inscriptions use twenty-four letters; most Scandinavian ones used only sixteen.

Ancient rune stones were memorials and signposts. Runic carvings on small objects were used as magical charms to heal a sickness or to ward off bad luck.

Crossing the Swedish border to Norway

For many centuries the Swedes were largely homogeneous. That means they were similar. Their parents and grandparents were all of the same ethnic descent.

Immigration

During and after World War II, people from other countries began to move to Sweden. Most of them came from Finland and other Nordic countries in search of job opportunities.

Citizens of the five Nordic countries can cross the borders of Sweden without passports or work permits. A citizen of a Nordic country can become a Swedish citizen after two years in residence. (Those from other nations becomes eligible for citizenship after five years of residence.)

Sweden needed more workers after the war. People from other European countries—beyond Scandinavia—came to work in Sweden. In recent years, refugees from other continents have also found homes in Sweden. Today about 13 percent of the people in Sweden were either born in other countries or have at least one parent born elsewhere.

Turkish immigrants are part of the Swedish culture.

All foreign citizens can vote in county and municipal council elections, and they can run for local offices if they have been a registered resident of Sweden for three years.

It is important to note that all noncitizens living in Sweden have the same rights to social benefits and education as Swedish citizens.

Ferries transport people between harbors in Sweden and Finland.

Minorities

Finns are the largest minority group in Sweden. It is easy to travel quickly from Helsinki and Turku, in Finland, to Sweden's Stockholm. Ferries crossing the Baltic Sea do a thriving business.

The history of the Swedish and Finnish people has been interrelated since the Middle Ages. Finland was a part of Sweden for nearly 600 years. Many people of Swedish descent live in

Persons per sq. mi.		Persons per sq. km.
more than 260		more than 100
130–260		50–100
25–130		10–50
3–25		1–10
fewer than 3		fewer than 1

Who Lives in Sweden?

Swedes	91%
Finns	3%
Other*	6%

*Sami and immigrants from the former Yugoslavia, Iran, Norway, Denmark, Turkey, Chile, and Poland

Finland. Some 320,000 people of Finnish descent live in Sweden today.

The Sami (Lapps) have been in northern Sweden longer than any other Swedish people and long before written records. The Sami and their reindeer were described in early Roman writings. Today there are about 17,000 Sami in Sweden. All together, in Norway, Sweden, Finland, and Russia, there are 50,000 to 60,000 Sami.

The Sami have their own language and preserve their own culture, but they have adapted to modern times. They are no longer nomads. They live in villages and towns and work at a variety of jobs besides reindeer herding. Many Sami men are miners or lumberjacks. Those who still herd reindeer use modern transportation and communication equipment to make their work easier.

Since the 1970s, Sweden has opened its doors to political refugees. New minority groups have become a part of the Swedish scene. More than 130,000 Swedish residents today have come from Chile, Iran, Turkey, and the former Yugoslavia. Some schools have students from up to a hundred different nations.

After centuries of living in an almost totally homogeneous society, Swedes—as well as the newcomers—now face challenges of adjustment to a new situation.

Populations of Major Swedish Cities (1993 est.)

Stockholm	684,576
Göteborg	444,553
Malmö	242,706
Uppsala	181,191
Linköping	130,489

Where the Swedes Live

There are about 8.8 million people in Sweden. It is one of the least densely populated nations in Europe. The overall average is fifty-one people per square mile (twenty per sq km). But more than half the country has fewer than twenty-five people per square mile (ten per sq km).

Four out of five people live in urban areas. About a third are in the metropolitan areas of Stockholm, Göteborg, and Malmö.

The Swedish government has subsidized new and modernized housing, so just about everyone has a comfortable place to live. About four out of ten people live in apartment

A modern apartment building in Kista

buildings, but the majority of families with children are in single- or two-family homes.

The Swedes are fond of getting close to nature. For this reason, it is every family's dream to have a summer home in the country. There are about 600,000 second homes in Sweden.

Language

Swedish is the official and common language of this nation. It is a Germanic language. Norwegian, Danish, and Icelandic are all similar to Swedish. The Sami and the Finnish-speaking Swedes in the north speak Swedish as well as their own first languages. Children of more recent immigrants learn Swedish in school. Many of them are also able to study the language of their parents in school.

Pronunciation Key

The Swedish language has three letters not used in English: å, ä, and ö.

- The å sounds like the "a" in "law."
- The ä is sometimes pronounced like the "e" in "get," sometimes like "a" in "hat."
- The ö is like the "u" in "fur," without the "r" sound.

Swedes use different tones to tell the difference between some similar words. Most non-Swedes have difficulty learning these subtle differences.

Common Swedish Words and Phrases

English	Swedish	Pronunciation
Good morning	*God morgon*	(goo morron)
Good night	*God natt*	(goo naht)
Yes	*Ja*	(yaa)
No	*Nej*	(nay)
Thank you	*Tack*	(tahk)
You're welcome	*Tack så mycket*	(tahk saw mewkar)
Excuse me	*Förlåt*	(fir LAWT)
Just a moment	*Ett ögonblick*	(eht urgonblik)
I understand	*Jag förstår*	(yaa FUR stawr)
I don't understand	*Jag förstår inte*	(yaa FUR stawr inta)

And it's okay to greet people by saying "hej" (pronounced "hay"). It's like "hi" in English.

English is also taught as a compulsory second language. Nearly everyone who was born in Sweden since World War II can speak English—many of them very well.

The Swedish language has letters and sounds that can be intimidating to English-speaking people.

Swedish Names

You may have noticed that many Swedish last names end in "son"—Andersson, Petersson, Olsson, Carlsson, and so forth. Until about a hundred years ago, family names did not exist in Sweden. If a man named Erik had a son named Carl, the boy would be called Carl Eriksson. A daughter in the family named Greta would be known as Greta Eriksdotter (*dotter* is Swedish for daughter).

Sometimes, however, family names were used that stood for the place the people lived in. Examples of this practice include *berg*, for hill, or *strand*, for shore.

This simple system worked out all right when people lived in small villages where most people knew each other. But as life became more complicated, family names came into common use.

Today so many Swedish names are similar, it is sometimes hard to find the person you are looking for. To help solve this problem, telephone directories list a person's occupation as well as his or her name.

CHAPTER FIVE

From the Vikings to the European Union

Many thousands of years ago, people in the country now known as Sweden lived off the land. They hunted wild game, fished in streams and lakes, and picked fruits and other plants for food. Some of them were nomads who herded flocks of small animals.

46

THROUGH MANY CENTURIES, THEY BEGAN to gather in small settlements. They planted crops and raised livestock. Prehistoric people lived as extended families, several generations together. As they met and intermarried with other families, clans developed. Clans grew into tribes, federations, and then provinces. Each province was independent, led by a local king.

These prehistoric people began to make tools of wood and stone, later of bronze and copper. They traveled and traded, exchanging furs for weapons and salt.

An eighth-century Viking ship

The Viking Period

By about A.D. 800 the Scandinavians—Swedes, Norwegians, and Danes—were traveling to many other parts of Europe. (Finland was not considered Scandinavian until much later.) The Swedes sailed to the east on the Baltic Sea, up rivers into Russia, and even as far as the Black and Caspian seas. The Danes went south to France, Spain, and Italy. The Norwegians sailed west, to the British Isles, Iceland, and even

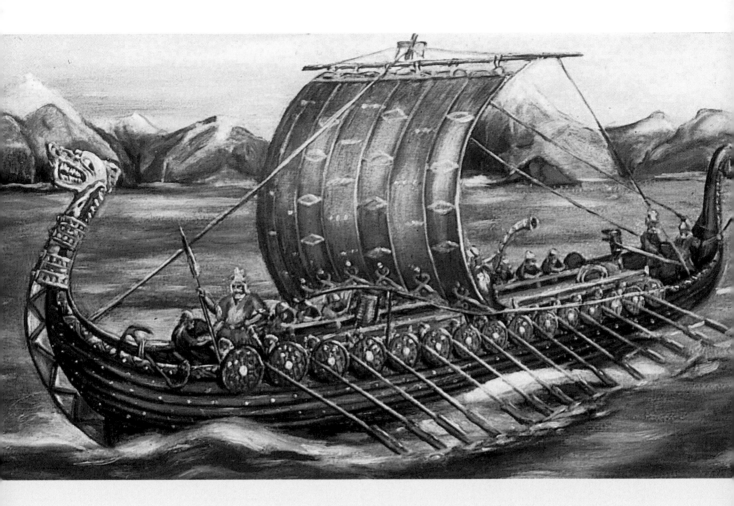

Viking Ships

The Vikings had no instruments, but they knew how to find their way across wide oceans by following the stars, observing currents, and looking for a few landmarks.

The unique design of Viking ships was as important as the Vikings' seamanship. The ships were long and narrow, with a sharp keel that helped them glide through the water with ease. Some were more than 100 feet (33 m) long and could travel as fast as 20 miles (32 km) per hour. The largest ones carried thirty-two oars, which were used to propel the ship when the winds were not right for sailing.

A Viking ship carried one huge square sail. During rainstorms, the sail could be lowered and fastened down to form a tentlike covering over the sailors and their possessions.

Often the ships were real works of art. The hulls were elaborately carved and painted. They swept upward in large, graceful curves toward pointed prows and sterns. The tip of the prow was usually decorated with the head of a dragon, serpent, horse, or other creature.

crossed the Atlantic Ocean to what is now Newfoundland, Canada. The Vikings, as they were called, were highly skilled shipbuilders and navigators.

Many of the Vikings were pirates and marauders, raiding and plundering the towns they passed through. Some were peaceful merchants—most of the time.

The stories of Viking adventures and exploits have often overshadowed the history of life back home in Scandinavia. When they were at home, Viking men lived with their families on farms. Women, children, and older people all shared in the farmwork. When the men went off to faraway lands, the others carried on.

A Viking minstrel singing to a gathering of townspeople

After the Vikings

There were three classes of society in Sweden in the Middle Ages—chieftains and minor kings, called Earls; peasants, called Karls; and slaves. Slavery was quite widespread. Most slaves were Swedish, not foreigners. Some of them were captured when a battle was lost. Some were people who voluntarily sold themselves into bondage in return for payment of their debts.

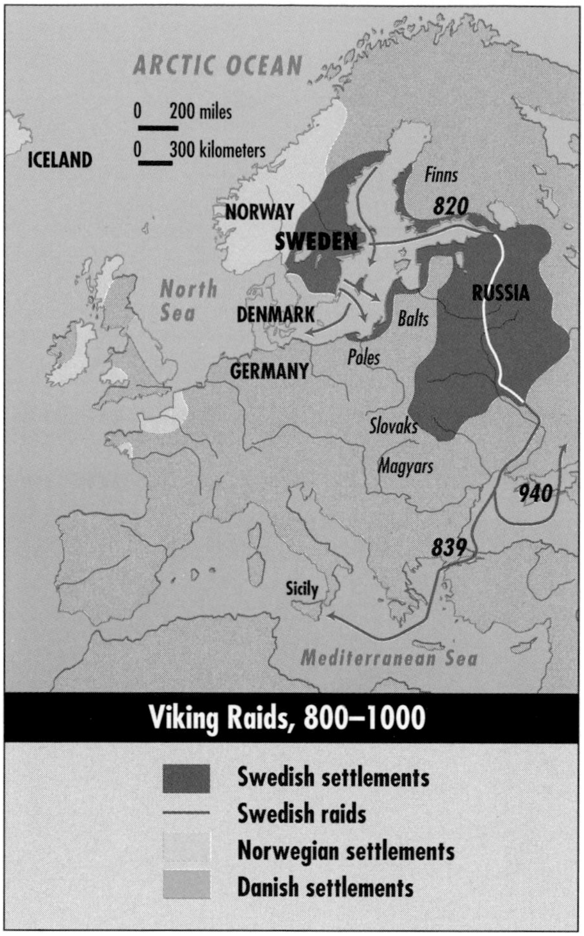
ARCTIC OCEAN
0 200 miles
0 300 kilometers
ICELAND
NORWAY
SWEDEN
Finns
820
RUSSIA
North Sea
DENMARK
Balts
Poles
GERMANY
Slovaks
Magyars
940
839
Sicily
Mediterranean Sea
Swedish settlements
Swedish raids
Norwegian settlements
Danish settlements

Viking Raids, 800–1000

Slaves had no rights—their masters could do whatever they wished with them. They could work them endlessly, torture them, even kill them as sacrifices to the ancient gods. Slavery was officially abolished in 1335, although it was not completely wiped out until quite some time later.

Free peasants governed themselves through a village association, the *byalag*. Tribes were headed by a council, or ting, and a local king or chieftain. Battles flared up frequently as the kings fought one another for power.

Christianity came to Sweden toward the end of the Viking period. Over time, the clergy became a powerful sector of the population, and the church acquired a lot of valuable property. A few aristocrats, merchants, and town burghers had a little status, but 95 percent of the people were peasants, the lowest class. They did all the work and paid taxes to the ruling classes.

Some of the coastal cities were engaged in active trade with other parts of the world. During the early Middle Ages, a group of German merchants formed the Hanseatic League. They controlled most of the trade in this region. Visby, on the island of Gotland, was one of their ports of call. The old city of Birka, in Upland, was another.

The kings and the church cooperated with each other. The king was not only recognized by the Roman Catholic Church, he was anointed and blessed in a religious ceremony. He was declared as ruler by the grace of God. In return, the king did not levy taxes on church properties.

Swedish settlers occupied Finland during this period, and the two countries were governed as one for 600 years.

The Folkung Dynasty

From 1250 to 1365, Sweden was ruled by members of the Folkung dynasty. The founder of this dynasty was a man

The tomb of Birger Jarl outside City Hall in Stockholm

named Birger Jarl. He was an advisor to a king, Eric, and hoped to be elected king when Eric died. His son was elected instead, but Birger was the power behind the throne. For more than a century, members of Birger Jarl's family held the throne.

The history of this family, known as the Folkung dynasty, is full of conspiracy and betrayal. Brothers and cousins battled, kidnapped, tortured, and murdered one another in their attempts to hold the throne.

The Black Death

A disastrous epidemic of the bubonic plague swept over Europe during the 1300s. About a third of the population in Scandinavia died as a result.

When a disease spreads over a large area, it is called a pandemic. Three pandemics of the plague are on record: one in the Mediterranean region in the 500s, the Black Death in Europe of the 1300s, and one that started in China in the mid-1800s.

The plague is rare in the world today, but isolated cases do occur. Effective methods of prevention and treatment have been developed.

One king had his wife crowned queen, the first time for such a celebration. Things must have been pretty unruly—the entire town burned down during the festivities.

Three brothers divided Sweden among themselves in 1310. Two years later, there was a huge royal double wedding. Two of the brothers married two young princesses from Norway.

In 1317, the third brother, Birger Magnusson, invited the others to a huge banquet. After the meal he had his guests seized and thrown into a dungeon. He declared himself to be the king of all Sweden. But these actions were too much for the dukes who had previously supported him. They rose up against Birger, and he left the country. The two brothers died in prison.

The nobles elected Birger's nephew, Magnus Eriksson, king. He was three years old. He inherited the crown of Norway as well, so the two countries, plus Finland, were united. Regents ran the affairs of state for the first thirteen years of his reign.

ARCTIC OCEAN

Lapland

Norwegian Sea

1655

1645

FINLAND

1617

NORWAY

SWEDEN

1561

RUSSIAN EMPIRE

North Sea

1645

Baltic Sea

1621

DENMARK *1658*

1648 *1648* *1629* POLAND

GERMAN STATES

1523–1683

	Sweden in 1523
	Colonization of Finland
	Acquisitions 1561–1683

ARCTIC OCEAN

Norwegian Sea

NORWAY (Denmark)

SWEDEN

RUSSIAN EMPIRE

North Sea

Baltic Sea

DENMARK

PRUSSIA

POLAND

1721–Present

| | Sweden in 1721 |
| —— | Current borders |

Magnus ruled for more than thirty years. He did a great deal to modernize the government, but he was faced with many severe difficulties. The regents had left the royal treasury empty, and when he was unable to pay his debts to the church, he was excommunicated. The Black Death wiped out a third of the country's population. A woman religious leader, Birgit Birgersdotter, criticized him harshly and did great harm to his reputation. The nobles overthrew him and sent him to prison in 1363.

The Stockholm Bloodbath

Union with Denmark and Norway

After a few years of rule by a German king, the council of advisors elected Margareta regent of Sweden. She was already the ruler of both Denmark and Norway. She reigned over the so-called Kalmar Union of the three nations.

The Union did not work very well after Margareta. In 1520, the Danish king Christian II ordered the murder of eighty-two of Sweden's leading citizens. This atrocity, known as the Stockholm Bloodbath, marked the end of Sweden's alliance with Denmark.

Margareta, Ruler of Three Kingdoms

Margareta of Denmark was a wise politician. She worked to have her son, Olaf, elected king of Denmark and Norway, and later Sweden. He was still a child, and he died before he could be crowned. Margareta was recognized as regent. Regents rule monarchies during the absence, disability, or minority of a king or queen.

Margareta worked hard to keep Scandinavia united and to strengthen the power of the monarchy. Because she had no heirs, she persuaded all three countries to select her grand-nephew Erik for their king. Erik was crowned at Kalmar in 1397. Margareta was the actual ruler for the next fifteen years.

This remarkable woman kept Scandinavia united and at peace. She encouraged economic and cultural growth and was generous to the church.

Margareta died in 1412, probably of the plague.

The Vasa Dynasty

Gustav Vasa lost his father and three other relatives in the Stockholm Bloodbath. He gathered supporters together to fight for freedom from Denmark. On June 6, 1523, the *Riksdag* (parliament) elected Gustav Vasa king of Sweden, and the anniversary is still celebrated as the country's National Day. The Riksdag also voted to establish a hereditary monarchy. That is, when a king or queen died, the crown would pass on to an heir.

Gustav I's grandson, Gustav II Adolph, is remembered as an able military and political leader who transformed Sweden into a great empire.

A statue of Gustav Vasa

Gustav II Adolph

Dynasties and Rulers of Sweden

Stenkil Dynasty	1061–1130	Erik of Pomerania	1396–1439	Gustavus Adophus	
		Engelbrekt (regent)	1435–1436	(Gustav II Adolph)	1611–1632
Dynasties of Sverker and of Erik		Karl Knutsson Bonde		Kristina	1632–1654
		(regent)	1438–1441		
Sverker I	1130–1156	Kristofer of Bavaria	1441–1448		
Erik the Holy (St. Erik)	1156–1160	Karl Knutsson Bonde	1448–1457	**Palatinate Dynasty**	
Magnus Henriksson	1160–1161	(regent)	1464–1465	Karl X Gustav	1654–1660
Karl Sverkersson	1161–1167		1467–1470	Karl XI	1660–1697
Kol and Burislev	1167–1169	Christian I	1457–1464	Karl XII	1697–1718
Knut Eriksson	1169–1195	Svante Nilsson Sture	1470–1497	Ulrika Eleonora	1719–1720
Sverker Karlsson	1195–1208	(regent)	1501–1503	Fredrik I of Hesse	1720–1751
Erik Knutsson	1208–1216	Hans	1497–1501		
Jon Sverkersson	1216–1222	Svante Nilsson Sture			
Erik Eriksson	1222–1229	(regent)	1504–1512	**Holstein-Gottorp Dynasty**	
	1234–1250	Sten Sture the Younger		Adolf Fredrik	1751–1771
Knut the Tall	1229–1234	(regent)	1512–1520	Gustav III	1771–1792
Birger Jarl (regent)	1248–1266	Christian II	1520–1521	Gustav IV Adolph	1792–1809
				Karl VIII	1809–1818
Folkung Dynasty		**Vasa Dynasty**			
Valdemar	1250–1275	Gustav Vasa (regent)	1521–1523	**Bernadotte Dynasty**	
Magnus Ladulås	1275–1290	(king)	1523–1560	Karl XIV Johan	1818–1844
Birger Magnusson	1290–1318	Erik XIV	1560–1568	Oskar I	1844–1859
Magnus Eriksson	1319–1364	Johan III	1568–1592	Karl XV	1859–1872
Albrecht		Sigismund	1592–1599	Oskar II	1872–1907
of Mecklenburg	1364–1389	Duke Karl (regent)	1592–1604	Gustav V	1907–1950
		Karl IX (Duke Karl)	1604–1611	Gustav VI Adolph	1950–1973
Danish Union and others				Carl XVI Gustav	1973–
Margareta	1389–1396				

The Vasa dynasty—Gustav and his descendants—led the country for nearly 200 years. Foreign investment was encouraged, as well as the arts and scholarship. The legal code and the educational system were reformed.

The last of the Vasas, Karl XII, tried to expand Sweden's power by military means. He fought a disastrous battle against Russia, which ended with 20,000 Swedish deaths. He lived in exile for a few years, then was killed in battle while trying to return to Sweden.

Liberty and Enlightenment

The people of Sweden were tired of unlimited royal power. A bloodless revolution followed the Vasa Era. A new constitution was adopted, transferring power from the monarch to the Riksdag. The king's (or queen's) powers were limited to the appointment of a twenty-four-member council of advisers.

Stockholm in the 1800s ("Street Scene in Stockholm" by Christoffer-Wilhelm Eckersberg, 1783–1853)

The 1700s saw much cultural, scientific, and economic progress. The population grew. Sweden even became a colonial power for a while. A joint Swedish and Dutch company established settlements in what is now the state of Delaware in 1638. Later called New Sweden, the colony was administered by Swedish governors from 1643 to 1655.

Sweden even ventured into the Caribbean. France gave Sweden the tiny island of St. Barthelmy in 1758, in return for trading rights in the port of Göteborg. It was Swedish for nearly a hundred years, but hardly any trace of Swedish culture can be found there today.

Toward the end of the period, however, political rivalry and problems with foreign relations weakened the government. A new, strong leader was needed.

Swedish-born Gustav III became king in 1771. He moved quickly to reestablish the power of the monarch. He encouraged cultural activities and founded the Swedish Academy of

From the Vikings to the European Union **57**

Literature, Music, Art, and History and Antiques. He was responsible for the building of the Royal Opera House and Royal Dramatic Theater in Stockholm.

The members of the aristocracy were worried about Gustav's increasing power. They plotted against him and had him assassinated during a masked opera ball. Later the composer Giuseppe Verdi used this incident as a plot in his opera *The Masked Ball.*

Opposite:
The Royal Opera House

The Nineteenth Century

Sweden was forced to surrender Finland to Russian czar Alexander in 1809, as a consequence of the Napoleonic wars. Norway, however, was united with Sweden under one king from 1814 to 1905.

The nineteenth century was a period of industrial development. Sweden had rich resources in mining and timber. Swedish engineers were

Karl XV, king of Sweden and Norway

developing new industrial products and consumer goods. New techniques were invented for processing wood and paper and for making steel.

Trade unions and cooperatives began to emerge. These organizations were interested in improving the standard of living for their members. They also promoted education and began to take an interest in politics. Several labor groups got together to organize the Social Democratic Party in 1889.

There were twice as many people in Sweden in 1900 as there had been a hundred years before. The population was growing faster than the nation's ability to feed its people. Between 1880 and 1930, more than a million people emigrated, mostly to North America.

Some Swedes made their way to North America.

Neutrality

From Viking days until nearly two hundred years ago, Sweden's history was a violent one. There were constant wars with other countries and bloody struggles for power among kings and princes. But since the early nineteenth century, the nation has been peaceful. The official policy is strict neutrality. This means Sweden will not take sides in other nations' conflicts. It has not joined any military alliances with other countries.

The union of Norway and Sweden ended peacefully in 1905. Most people in Scandinavia were very poor as the twentieth century dawned. The Industrial Revolution caused unemployment and poverty at first, but rapid development of the nation's industries soon proved to be a benefit. World War I created new markets for Swedish products.

Parliamentary government was adopted in Sweden in 1917. Laws soon followed to create a modern constitutional democracy. All adults gained the right to vote in 1921. From time to time, there have been movements to do away with the monarchy, but it has survived.

A few years later, the Great Depression swept across the world. Many Swedes were out of work. In 1932, the Social Democratic Party was the victor in national elections. It has been the most important political power in Sweden ever since. The new government began to take measures to improve living conditions for the people. Many welfare programs were planned, but most of them were not put into practice until after World War II.

Sweden's Parliament

Unemployed workers filling out questionnaires during the Great Depression

Sweden became part of
the European Union in 1995.

Sweden was able to stay neutral throughout that war. Its next-door neighbors were not so fortunate. Finland declared war on Russia, and both Norway and Denmark were occupied by Germany. Refugees from several countries near the Baltic Sea were able to find safe haven in Sweden. This nation has worked actively for the cause of world peace ever since it joined the United Nations in 1946.

Sweden's economy grew and diversified rapidly during the postwar years. The people enjoyed a high standard of living, and the state's welfare programs spread the wealth across the population.

In recent years, however, high taxes, inflation, and environmental pollution have plagued the nation. Control has swung back and forth among various coalitions of the leading political parties.

A hotly debated matter was the decision to join the European Union (EU). A referendum was held, and Sweden became a full member of the EU on January 1, 1995. The government emphasized that Sweden would continue to be militarily neutral and therefore would not join the North Atlantic Treaty Organization (NATO). Sweden also intends to use its EU status to promote free trade and foster closer cooperation with its Baltic neighbors, Estonia, Latvia, and Lithuania.

A People's Government

Sweden has a king and queen. They are Carl Gustav XVI and his wife, Queen Silvia. They live in a castle. An Act of Succession took effect in 1980, stating that the throne is to be inherited by the oldest child of the king and queen, whether male or female. Crown Princess Victoria, born in 1977, is in line to inherit the throne from her father.

The royal family: (standing left to right) Carl Philip, King Carl, Crown Princess Victoria, Madeleine, and (seated) Queen Silvia

S WEDEN IS A LIMITED CONSTITUTIONAL MONARCHY. That means that the king or queen has only ceremonial powers. King Carl presides at the opening of the Riksdag each year. He is the symbolic and formal representative of the nation on other special occasions.

The real power in Sweden belongs to the people, through their elected representatives in the Riksdag.

The Riksdag has been Sweden's legislative body since the fifteenth century. It follows an ancient tradition. During the Middle Ages the *ting* (tribal council) ran the local government.

The Monarchy

In Viking times, Swedish kings were elected by the ting. This practice continued for a number of centuries. Several times a powerful king would try to establish a dynasty. That is, he wanted to keep the throne in his own family, or at least the right to name his successor.

Crown Princess Victoria on her eighteenth birthday in 1995

Sweden's Great Seal

Kings, nobles, and important families in ancient times all had their own coats of arms, or family shields. These were displayed on personal possessions as marks of ownership.

The phrase "coat of arms" dates from the Middle Ages. At that time, the family shield was sewn on coats or capes that knights wore over their armor.

Certain designs were also recognized as symbols of kingdoms or nations. The Swedish symbol has included a lion and three crowns since the days of the Folkung dynasty. The total design changed often as new kings or dynasties came into power.

In 1908, the present Swedish Great Seal was made official. It shows a pair of lions holding up a smaller seal against a background of white ermine and red velvet. At the top is a large crown.

But members of the family didn't always get along. They would fight among themselves over the crown. Then the ting, and later the Riksdag, would step in and elect a new king.

The power has shifted between the monarch and the Riksdag over the centuries. In 1709, a constitution was adopted that limited the king's powers. He could only appoint the twenty-four members of a council of advisors. Lawmaking was up to the Riksdag.

A hundred years later another constitution gave the king executive power, but divided the legislative responsibility between the monarch and the Riksdag.

In 1810, Jean Bernadotte, a French general, was elected crown prince. He later became King Karl XIV Johan. His descendants have been Sweden's monarchs ever since. Their powers, however, have lessened. In 1917, the Riksdag took over legislative functions.

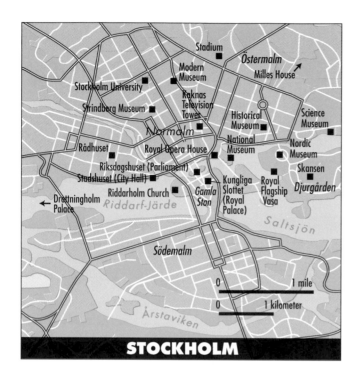

STOCKHOLM

Political posters for the Communist
and Right Wing parties

Until 1975, the king still appointed governmental ministers and presided over the cabinet. A new constitution took away this last political privilege. It established the monarch as the ceremonial head of state only. All governmental powers now are in the hands of the Riksdag and the cabinet.

The Riksdag

The principle of democracy has existed in Sweden since Viking days. Four groups—the nobles, clergy, burghers, and peasants—were represented in the Riksdag during the late Middle Ages. A reorganization about 150 years ago formed two houses of government.

The constitution of 1975 changed the Riksdag to a unicameral (one-house) parliament, elected by the people. It is responsible for passing laws and for selecting leaders to run the nineteen departments of the government.

The Riksdag is in session from October to May each year. One of its first duties after an election is to select

a prime minister. Usually, but not always, the person chosen is the leader of the political party that has won the most votes.

Elections to seats in the parliament are normally held every three years. All citizens aged eighteen or over can vote. Citizens of other nations who have lived in Sweden for three years can vote in local, but not national, elections.

The Riksdag has 349 members. Most of them represent geographic districts, or constituencies. Thirty-nine of the members are chosen differently. These seats are distributed among the various political parties, in proportion to the total number of votes cast for each party.

Sweden has five major political parties and several minor ones. The major parties are the Center, Moderate, Liberal, Social Democrats, and Greens (an environmental party). Since the late 1920s, the Social Democrats have been the party most often in power.

Swedish people take their right to vote very seriously. An election attracts nearly 90 percent of eligible voters to the polls.

Sweden's court system consists of a Supreme Court, Supreme Administrative Court, Labor Court, District Courts, and Courts of Appeal.

Local Government

Sweden is divided into counties and municipalities for local government purposes. As of 1995, there were 288 municipal governments and 23 county council areas. The central government appoints county governors. Local councils are elected by the people on the same day as national elections.

Local governments are responsible for collecting taxes. They also supervise the administration of national programs. These include education, public transportation, and health care.

The Middle Way

Sweden is sometimes admired among nations for having found a "middle way" between capitalism and socialism. Very few Swedish industries are nationalized, and private enterprise thrives. The Social Democratic party has not tried to take an active role in industry. Rather, it concentrates on providing social benefits for the citizens.

Lyrics to National Anthem

Thou ancient, thou free, thou mountain-crested North,
　Thou still, thou joyful, thou beauteous land!
　　I greet thee, fairest land on earth,
　Thy sun, thy sky, thy meadows green,
　Thy sun, thy sky, thy meadows green.

Thou rest on memories from the great days of old,
　When honored thy name swept around the world.
　　I know that thou art and remain what thou were.
　Yes, I want to live, I want to die in the North!
　Yes, I want to live, I want to die in the North!

The Swedish people believe that all citizens are entitled to a certain standard of living. This includes guaranteed medical and dental care, pensions, education, and many other services. People who cannot work because of sickness, injury, or unemployment receive allowances. In spite of high taxes to pay for these benefits, the general standard of living in Sweden is one of the highest in the world.

Along with private industry and government, cooperatives and strong labor unions are important elements in the

Sweden boasts a thriving medical system.

The Swedish Flag

Sweden's national flag is a horizontal yellow cross on a deep blue background. The intersection of the cross is to the left of center.

The flags of all five Nordic countries have a similar design, but in different colors. Denmark's is a white cross on a red background; Finland's is a light blue cross on white. Iceland and Norway each have a narrower cross within a white cross against the background. Iceland's is red within white on dark blue; Norway's is blue within white on red.

The similarity of these flags symbolizes the shared history of the five nations and their conversion to Christianity during the Middle Ages.

Sweden's blue and yellow flag was first used in the 1400s. It was flown by the nation's naval fleet in the

1500s. At that time it was a three-tongued pennant rather than a rectangle.

The current design became the official national emblem in 1663. A law passed in 1906 specified the correct proportions.

Manufacturing is an important part of the Swedish economy.

middle way. Co-ops are businesses that are owned jointly by individual producers or employees. Swedish co-ops are strong in manufacturing as well as in wholesale and retail distribution of products.

Relationships between labor unions and industry in Sweden have usually been very good. Both sides realize that a strong economy is needed in order to support successful social welfare programs.

Ombudsmen

Sweden has a governmental department that exists to represent the interests of private citizens. The officials of this department are called ombudsmen. The Riksdag established the Office of the Swedish Parliamentary Ombudsmen (JO) in 1809. Since then several other countries have copied the idea. Finland, Denmark, Norway, New Zealand, Great Britain, and Japan have similar systems.

Ombudsmen listen to complaints from citizens about actions or decisions by governmental agencies or officials. They are empowered to investigate any situation they feel needs to be looked into and to take disciplinary action when necessary.

The purpose of the ombudsmen system is to protect the rights of individuals in their contacts with authorities. Some of the areas of special interest are consumer affairs, equal opportunity, ethnic discrimination, and the rights of children and disabled persons.

Women have a strong presence in Sweden.

Equality of Women

Women have achieved more equality in Scandinavian countries than in many others. It comes from a long tradition. Birger Jarl wrote laws in the thirteenth century that guaranteed protection for women. He also wrote a law giving women inheritance rights.

Scandinavians also point to the Viking heritage to explain their tradition. During those times, women had to run the families, farms, and village affairs when their husbands went to sea.

Equal voting rights for all adults came to Sweden in 1921. Women can run for all political offices and enter any occupation they choose. In 1980, an Act of Equality made equal rights for women an official policy. Almost all Swedish women work outside the home. They are doctors, mechanics, airline pilots, designers. There are even women in the once all-male Lutheran clergy.

When a new baby is born, the mother is given 360 days leave from her job, still receiving 90 percent of her salary. An additional ninety days leave is possible, at less pay.

If the couple wishes, all or part of that paid leave can be taken by the father instead. In either case, the job must be held for the parent to return to work.

An efficient day-care system allows Swedish women to remain in the working society.

Legislation providing day care for children and other social benefits help give women an equal position in society. Observers of Swedish society have pointed out, however, that women still perform much more than half the family's household chores. Also, there are very few women in top positions in industry. They have made more progress toward full equality in political life than in the workplace.

The Nordic Council

Sweden, Finland, Norway, Denmark, and Iceland function in many ways as if they were a single large nation. This is made possible largely through the work of the Nordic Council of Ministers.

Each year the presidents and other leaders of the five member countries meet face to face to discuss possible solutions to common problems. Subjects of concern include environmental protection, education, scientific research, industry, and energy.

Citizens of all five countries can move freely throughout the region without visas or passports. They do not need work permits to take jobs in other Nordic nations. When living in one of these countries, they are entitled to most of the same privileges as citizens.

Dag Hammarskjöld

Dag Hammarskjöld was born in 1905. His family had been prominent soldiers and statesmen for 300 years. His father was prime minister of Sweden while Dag was a boy. Hammarskjöld had many talents and interests. He enjoyed skiing and mountain climbing and was an excellent gymnast. He spoke English, French, and German fluently.

After graduating from the University of Uppsala, Dag went into government service. He soon demonstrated a talent for diplomacy; he negotiated Sweden's first trade agreement with Great Britain. He became assistant foreign minister, then minister of state for foreign affairs.

In 1952, Hammarskjöld was vice chairman of the Swedish delegation to the United Nations. Only a year later he was elected secretary-general of the international organization. While in office he worked to broaden the role of the UN in international diplomacy. His philosophy was "preventive diplomacy."

Dag Hammarskjöld was killed in an airplane crash on his way to try to help resolve problems in central Africa. Later that year, 1961, he was awarded the Nobel prize for peace — the first person to be so honored after death.

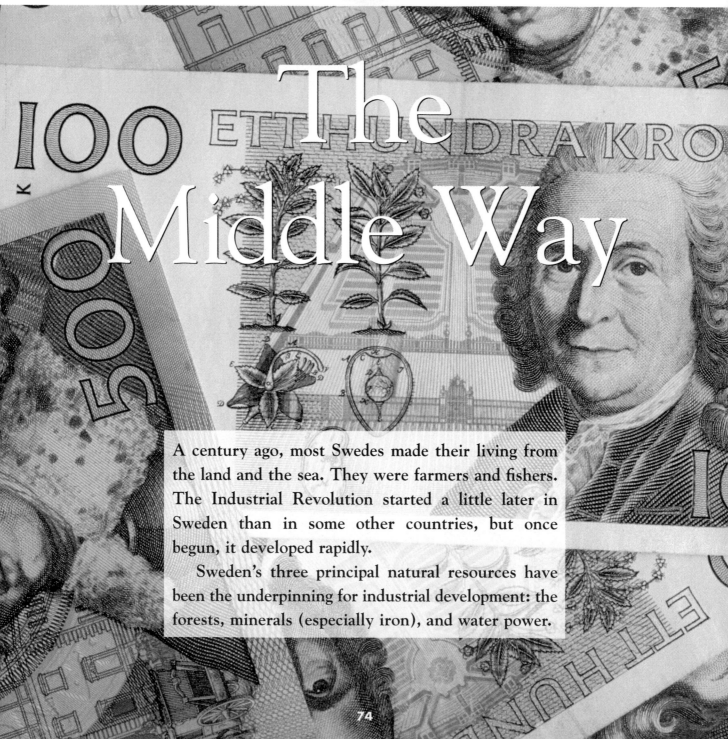

The Middle Way

A century ago, most Swedes made their living from the land and the sea. They were farmers and fishers. The Industrial Revolution started a little later in Sweden than in some other countries, but once begun, it developed rapidly.

Sweden's three principal natural resources have been the underpinning for industrial development: the forests, minerals (especially iron), and water power.

C HANGES IN THE ECONOMY BROUGHT about changes in population patterns. Rural people moved from villages to larger towns where they could find jobs. Jobs also attracted immigrants from other countries.

Sweden's economy has been described as "the middle way" between capitalism and socialism. In terms of ownership, it is far from socialistic—more than 85 percent of industry is privately owned. Cooperatives and public agencies own the rest.

An oil refinery

Cooperatives

The cooperative movement is very strong in the Nordic countries. Co-ops, as they are usually called, are businesses or other organizations owned and managed by the workers or members. There are manufacturing co-ops in Sweden that make such products as paper and clothing. Agricultural co-ops make it possible for farmers to pool their resources to purchase heavy equipment and get their goods to market. Most of Sweden's milk, meat, and dairy products are sold through co-ops.

Some artists have their own co-ops.

Opposite: **Sorting logs at a pulp factory**

Some apartment buildings are cooperatively owned, also. Artists and craftspeople have their own co-ops.

Another way to describe the Swedish economy is to call it "humane capitalism." Private industry, government, and labor work closely together. Responsibility for such matters as productivity, research and development, worker's welfare, social legislation, and protection of the environment is shared by all sectors.

Control of private industry in Sweden is highly concentrated. Major firms are headed by a few family dynasties. There are checks and balances in the system, however.

The Swedish society has always stressed discipline, efficiency, and good organization. These characteristics and a high level of education, along with cooperation among different interests, have helped Sweden to achieve one of the highest standards of living in the world.

Since World War II, Sweden has made a name for itself in the world market that is quite amazing for a nation with such a small population. One reason is that Swedish manufacturers have always stressed high quality of products. Another is a willingness to invest heavily in research and development of new products and methods.

Forestry

More than half of Sweden's land is covered by forests. People have depended on them for many things.

Birch trees, with their snow-white bark, beautify the countryside of southern Sweden. Northern forests are primarily evergreens. Birch wood was not used commercially until recently, now one-eighth of wood pulp produced in Sweden is birch.

At first, wood was cut from the forests primarily for fuel. Charcoal was made for the mining industry, and some raw lumber was exported. Then sawed timber became an increasingly important export. Later, the emphasis was on production of wood pulp for papermaking. Today, Sweden is the world's third largest exporter of pulp and paper products.

Pulp and paper are manufactured by some of Sweden's largest industrial groups. By contrast, about five hundred small sawmills produce almost all of Sweden's sawed timber.

Modern machinery and transportation have made the pulp and paper

What Sweden Grows, Makes, and Mines

Agriculture

Sugar beets	2,349 metric tons
Barley	1,660 metric tons
Wheat	1,518 metric tons

Livestock *(in number of live animals)*

Pigs	2,328,405
Cattle	1,826,489
Sheep	483,428

Manufacturing	Percentage of all manufacturing output
Machinery and transport equipment	34%
Paper and paper products	12%
Food and beverages	9%
Wood and wood products	4%
Textiles and wearing apparel	1%

Mining

Iron ore	19.3 million metric tons
Copper	332,600 metric tons
Lead	123,100 metric tons

industry much more efficient. But one problem has not been completely solved—the unpleasant sulphur smell of manufacturing these products. An environmental policy law was passed in 1988, and Swedish industry is working with the government to reduce hazardous emissions into the air, waterways, and soil.

Swedish people are very sensitive to environmental protection. The nation has one of the best and most effective paper-recycling programs in Europe.

Sweden has an effective recycling program.

One wood product that can be found in almost everyone's home in the United States and Canada was invented by a Swede. Can you guess what it might be? It's very small, but it would be hard to imagine getting along without it.

Gustav Pasch, a Swedish chemist, invented the safety match in 1844. That's the match that can only be lighted when it is scratched across a special surface. A Swedish manufacturer

began to produce huge quantities of these matches a few years later, and Sweden soon became a world leader in producing and exporting matches. Today the center for this industry is the town of Jönköping, on Lake Vättern.

Swedish Inventions

Besides Gustav Pasch's safety match (left) and the dynamite that Alfred Nobel invented, here are a few other widely used and well-known products invented by Swedes: Ball bearings, the implantable pacemaker, the Celsius thermometer, the screw propeller, the zipper, the adjustable wrench, the Hasselblad camera, and Styrofoam.

There are laws in Sweden against lighting fires out of doors—whether one uses matches or any other means—during summer months. Forest fires are a great hazard during long, dry, summer periods.

Mining

Copper was mined in Falun, in the province of Dalarna, more than a thousand years ago. During the seventeenth century, when Sweden was in its heyday as a world power, other minerals were discovered in the region. A broad belt of minerals lies beneath central Sweden, from east to west. The abundance of hydropower, plus wood for charcoal, were great assets for the booming mining industry.

More than three hundred different minerals have been discovered in the region. Most of them are not plentiful enough to mine. Copper has not been mined commercially in Falun for the past few years, but the town attracts many tourists. Guided tours of the mine, an 1882 wire rolling mill, and a mining museum tell the story of the area's active past.

The world's richest iron ore seam lies in the far north of Sweden. Geologist Hjalmar Lundbohm had heard stories about local iron ore finds near Kiruna. About a hundred years ago he came to the area. Only Sami lived in the region. The iron deposits he discovered have been mined for the last century. Geologists believe there is enough iron there to last for another two hundred years.

Sweden also has deposits of zinc, silver, gold, tungsten, and uranium. Small amounts of coal are mined in Skåne, but only enough for local uses.

Agriculture

In 1880, three out of four people in Sweden were agricultural workers. Today only about 3 percent make a living from farming. Only about 10 percent of Sweden's land is suitable for farming.

The climate for agriculture is far better in Skåne and other southern regions than in the rest of the country. Principal crops are wheat, potatoes, sugar beets, and fodder for livestock. Farmers raise dairy cows and beef cows, pigs, poultry, and sheep.

About two-thirds of the farms in Sweden are small and individually owned. Nearly all the farmers belong to agricultural cooperatives. The co-ops process and market the farm products.

A Metric Nation— Almost!

Sweden uses the metric system, but some old local measures are still in use, notably the Swedish mile (10 kilometers).

Opposite: **Copper mining is among Sweden's many industries.**

Products manufactured in Sweden are known around the world. Two automobile manufacturers turn out cars that are sold everywhere— Volvo and Saab. Both have excellent reputations for high quality. Volvo is the largest industrial company in the nation. Saab is a part of Saab-Scania, which also manufactures trucks, buses, and aircraft.

Sweden is said to be the most motorized country in Europe, with one car for every three people.

The Ericsson Company, also in Sweden, has been manufacturing telephones since the 1880s. A world leader in production of mobile phones, Ericsson has always been on the cutting edge in communications. A single telephone system serves all the Nordic countries. More telephones per capita—including mobile phones—are owned in this part of the world than in any other.

Electrolux is the world's largest producer of household appliances. Sweden is among the world's leading shipbuilding nations. Swedish steel products include stainless sheet, structural, roller bearing, and high-speed cutting steel.

An Ericsson plant

Chemicals and Pharmaceuticals

The chemical industry is one of Sweden's major employers. Rubber, plastics, industrial and medical gases, and paints are some of the products.

Pharmaceuticals make up 2 percent of the country's industrial production. Most of the products are exported. The industry is active in many areas of medical and drug research,

Opposite: **A Volvo manufacturing plant**

Swedish Currency

The krona is the basic unit of currency in Sweden. It is commonly abbreviated as "kr" or "SEK." The plural is kronor. One krona equals 100 öre.

Paper currency comes in values of 10, 20, 50, 100, 500, 1,000, and 10,000 kronor. Coins are for 50 öre and for 1, 5, and 10 krona.

Elements from nature and symbols from Sweden's Great Seal are used on coins: the lion rampant and the three crowns. Bills carry the picture of some of Sweden's most famous people, such as Jenny Lind, an internationally famous concert singer of the nineteenth century known as the "Swedish nightingale," and the scientist Carolus Linnaeus.

Alfred Nobel

Born in 1833, Alfred Nobel grew up to become one of the most successful businessmen in the history of Sweden. His name is still recognized around the world: Alfred Nobel, benefactor of the famous Nobel prizes. In his will, he left great sums of money to be used for awards given each year to individuals who "have conferred the greatest benefit on mankind."

Nobel spent most of his early years in Russia, where he got an excellent education. Like his father, his main interest was in chemistry. He spoke five languages and traveled in Europe and the United States while still in his teens.

When he was twenty years old, Alfred went back to Sweden with his parents. His two brothers stayed in Russia to run the family businesses.

Alfred developed great skills as a scientist, inventor, and businessman. His most famous invention, dynamite, revolutionized mining and road construction. (Nobel's final laboratory is shown on p. 85.) He worked in other areas too, such as synthetics and telecommunications.

During his lifetime, Nobel patented more than 350 of his inventions. He founded nearly a hundred multinational companies, spread around the world on five continents.

Alfred Nobel's life and work are full of contradictions. He stated that war is a horror and a crime, yet much of his fortune came from the manufacture and sale of armaments. He enjoyed great financial success and acclaim, but was a rather lonely, melancholy man who never married.

The Nobels believed in taking good care of their employees. Few other employers of the time provided the benefits Nobels' workers enjoyed. Accidents at the dynamite

factory in Karlskoga, however, have caused many injuries and deaths over the years.

While he was still alive, Alfred Nobel began giving away great sums of money to help people in need. Then he signed a will, putting most of his fortune in a fund to finance the Nobel prizes. Each year, Swedish committees award generous cash prizes to outstanding individuals in the categories of physics, chemistry, physiology or medicine, and literature. Since 1968 another category, economics, has been awarded in Nobel's memory by the Central Bank of Sweden.

Nobel Prize for Peace: Most Coveted of All

Alfred Nobel decided that the winner of the prize for peace should be chosen by a committee of the Norwegian Parliament. This prize, probably the most coveted and admired of all, is for "the best work for fraternity between nations, for the abolition or reduction of standing armies and for the holding of peace conferences."

In 1982, a Swedish sociologist, Alva Myrdal (left), was co-winner of the prize. She had worked for many years for the cause of military disarmament. It is ironic that the money for the prize comes from the armament industry whose size she wanted to cut.

such as cancer, eye diseases, growth disorders, and dialysis. Astra, an internationally notable pharmaceutical company, is doing research in gastrointestinal, respiratory, and cardiovascular diseases.

Other companies are working in the fields of plant breeding and animal husbandry.

Transportation

All major cities and towns in Sweden are served by Scandinavian Airlines (SAS) and its affiliates. This airline is jointly owned by Danish, Norwegian, and Swedish companies. SAS was the first airline company to fly over the North Pole. This route, from Sweden to Japan by way of Anchorage, Alaska, cut flying time between the two countries by twenty hours.

Scandinavian Airlines (SAS) serves all of Sweden.

Sweden has a good railroad network, mostly electrified. The spacious railroad cars are equipped with modern conveniences. Primarily owned by the government, the network covers the entire country. The Inland Railway has a beautiful, 800-mile (1,300-km) route along the "spine" of Sweden from north to south. This is popular with tourists. They can buy a ticket that is good for ten days with unlimited stops along the route.

The Inland Railway

This ferry connects Sweden to Denmark.

Dozens of ferry lines connect Sweden with Denmark, Germany, and Finland.

Sweden has a good highway system linking all parts of the nation. A network of express bus services makes travel to all major towns and cities easy.

The World Market

Swedish industries are very active in the world market. The government encourages foreign investment in Swedish industries. At the same time, Swedish investors have interests in many multinational companies based elsewhere.

As one Swedish business leader says, "We can't depend simply on our market here at home. We don't have enough people. We have to go worldwide."

At the end of the twentieth century, economies are changing rapidly all over the world. This is especially true in Europe. In 1995, Sweden became a member of the European Union (EU). Eventually all member nations will have to make sure their laws and policies conform to the standards and treaties of the EU. It is too soon to say just how this alliance will affect the Swedish economy, but expectations are high.

Unions

Four out of five Swedish workers, including professional employees, belong to trade unions. The unions in turn belong to one of three labor groups: the Swedish Trade Union Confederation, Confederation of Professional Employees, and Confederation of Professional Associations. Employers in the private sector have their own organization, the Swedish Employers' Confederation.

Pay bargaining is decentralized. It is conducted between the employers' federation and the union or at the individual company level. Strikes are uncommon. The government promotes full employment and provides training programs for people in

A Railroad for Iron Ore

The iron mines in the far northern part of Sweden needed a way to transport their ore to markets. During the nineteenth century, rail lines were built to Luleö, a port on the Baltic Sea. That was fine for part of the year, but during many months the harbor was blocked with ice. Huge icebreakers were brought in, but they could not clear the waters enough for ships to sail.

Toward the end of the century, Swedish engineers were able to plan a railway that would go right across the top of mountains into Norway. The line went all the way to the ice-free port of Narvik, on the Atlantic coast. Soon long trains of cars, filled with the valuable Swedish iron ore, were rolling over the mountain range.

Passengers are carried on this route, also. Tourists make the trip to enjoy the scenery. Hikers use the trains to reach the area. There are many hiking trails and mountain cabins along the range.

need of work. Unions and employers in Sweden have worked together to improve safety and working conditions.

Labor Laws

Several laws in Sweden protect employees from unfair practices on the part of employers. Employees have the right to take part in a union-approved strike. They can have representatives on company boards of directors. They are entitled to take leaves of absence for educational purposes. Discrimination based on sex is forbidden. Employers must negotiate with unions before making major changes. Employees' jobs are protected; there must be very strong reasons for firing anyone.

The Work Environment Act regulates working conditions, including safety and health. A normal work week is forty hours, and paid vacation time is a minimum of five weeks.

Religious Beliefs and Practices

Centuries ago, most people in the world were polytheists. That means they believed in many gods, not just one. Polytheistic religions are also called pagan.

The ancients believed the gods were responsible for acts of nature, such as wind, rain, and sunshine. The gods held the answers to many questions. Would the crops grow well this summer? Would this newly married couple have many sons? Would these warriors be triumphant in battle? Would the seas be calm and the winds steady so ships could sail safely home?

Viking Gods

THE VIKINGS HAD SEVERAL MAJOR GODS. These gods lived in a place called Asgard. Odin was the chief over all of the others. In some stories handed down through generations, the name Odin also seems to refer to the king. Odin was the god of war, magic, and wisdom.

Frey was the god of marriage and fertility. Prayers and sacrifices were offered to Frey for success in growing crops and in producing children. Frey's sister Freyja was the goddess of love.

Odin's son Thor ruled over the skies. He created rain, wind, and thunder. The Vikings explained to their children that thunder was caused when Thor rode his chariot through the heavens. There are many tales about Thor's adventures. He was always victorious over enemies. A magic hammer and a magic belt helped him get the best of giants, trolls, and elves. Loki was a mischief-maker. He loved to think up tricks to play on the other gods.

Odin: the Norse god, with his two crows, Hugin (thought) and Munin (memory)

Thor: the Norse god, fishing for the serpent of Midgard, from the boat of the giant Hymir

Religious Beliefs and Practices   **91**

A Viking funeral. The body was placed in a ship, set on fire, and sent out to sea. ("The Funeral of a Viking," 1893, by Sir Frank Dicksee, 1853–1928)

The Vikings also believed in life after death. Valhalla was a place for men who died gloriously in battle. When they died, Odin's daughters, called the Valkyries, would take them to Valhalla. Once there, the warriors enjoyed a life of endless bliss, filled with eating, drinking, and fighting.

Bodies of the slain warriors were buried. Their important possessions were buried with them. Sometimes survivors would place a Viking's body in his ship, which was then set afire and sent out to sea.

Niflheim was the Viking word for "the other world." Hel, in Niflheim, meant land of the dead, but it was not the same as the Christian concept of hell.

Stories about the Viking gods were passed from village to village and tribe to tribe. They were well known all over Scandinavia. Viking gods were also known in some of the European countries where Vikings settled.

The religion was not a structured, organized institution. Customs varied from one place to another. Worship celebrations were held outdoors. These were mostly bloody, cruel rites. Both animals and people were sacrificed—killed—as offerings to the gods.

The Vikings were fond of jewelry. They made lucky charms of gold and silver. A favorite design was copied after Thor's hammer. Children and adults wore these amulets to protect themselves from evil.

Christianity

Christianity was spreading over Europe toward the end of the Viking period. Vikings and Christians began to intermarry. When rulers adopted Christianity, the people had to follow,

Saint Birgit

Birgit Birgersdotter was a remarkable and controversial woman of the fourteenth century. Some call her the Swedish Joan of Arc.

Birgit was born into an aristocratic family. She was very religious and had her first vision while still a child. Married at age thirteen, she had eight children. Her husband became an advisor to King Magnus Eriksson and Birgit was lady-in-waiting to the queen.

Birgit and her husband decided to work for the church, but he died when she was in her forties. After that, she had many visions and wrote about them. The seven volumes she wrote are an important part of medieval history.

Believing that God was speaking to her directly, Birgit tried to influence the king to try to stop the Hundred Years' War. When he did not follow her advice, she publicly attacked his morals.

Birgit lived the last half of her life in Italy, where she continued to write about her revelations and to work with the sick and the poor. She also traveled to other countries and tried to influence many political leaders. She encouraged the revolt against King Magnus. These activities greatly increased both her popularity and unpopularity.

Several miracles were attributed to Birgit, and she was canonized in 1391.

Easter Saturday

On Easter Saturday in Sweden, young girls dress like witches, smearing their faces with paint and dirt and donning long skirts and head scarves. Carrying broomsticks, pots, and kettles, they go from door to door around the neighborhood. The neighbors are expected to throw small coins into the pots and kettles. The practice is similar to the Halloween tradition in other countries.

People in Sweden believed that at Easter all the witches would mount their broomsticks and fly away to join the devil on Blåkulla (Blue Mountain). People set off firecrackers to scare the witches away.

Today's customs poke fun at the superstitions that at one time resulted in cruelty to women accused of witchcraft.

and the old beliefs began to die out. Some people hung on to the old ideas while gradually accepting the Roman Catholic faith. Some ancient stone carvings display symbols of both the old and new religions.

The first Christian missionary came to Sweden in the ninth century. The first Christian king ruled in the tenth and eleventh centuries. The clergy became more and more influential. They founded schools, opposed the institution of slavery, and encouraged the arts.

During the 1500s, King Gustav Vasa encouraged Protestantism. He seized the property of the Catholic Church and decreed that the Lutheran Church was Sweden's official religious organization.

Opposite: **An ancient Swedish church**

Below: **The Lutheran Church became Sweden's official religious organization.**

Religious Holidays

Celebrations to mark the changing of the seasons have been held since prehistoric times. Some Christian holidays and festivals have certain traditions that date from pagan celebrations.

The Christmas season in Sweden lasts from December 13 to January 6 (Twelfth Night) or even until January 13 (Saint Knut's Day). It begins with St. Lucia's Day, named for a young girl who was martyred during Roman times. Young girls get up early and dress in long white gowns. One girl in each household, class, club, or factory is named the Lucia, and she wears a crown of candles (left). There are parades and parties everywhere, and candles provide light and decorations. Christmas trees are decorated with ornaments, mostly made of straw. Straw goats are popular; they stand for the old god Thor. Presents are delivered and hidden by Jultomten, the Christmas elf. The whole Christmas season is called the Festival of Light. It is also called Yuletide. The Vikings also held a celebration at this time of year, welcoming light to the time when the days were the shortest.

Easter is celebrated as a religious holiday, but also as a time for hunting Easter eggs. This custom is another reminder of a Viking festival, when children hunted for wild birds' eggs.

Religion in Sweden

Eighty-eight percent of Swedes are members of the Lutheran Church. Lutheranism is the state religion of Sweden, with the Archbishopric at Uppsala. The monarch and cabinet members dealing with church matters must be members of the Lutheran Church. The Swedish constitution, however, protects religious freedoms, and, according to a 1991 estimate, there were 147,414 Roman Catholics; 95,800 members of the Pentecostal Church; 77,013 members of the Mission Covenant Church of Sweden; 26,600 members of the Salvation Army; 21,000 Baptists; and 15,000 to 20,000 Jews.

People in many parts of the world had believed in witches since ancient times. In the 1600s and 1700s, this belief became an obsession in much of Europe, and in North America as well. Many innocent women were accused of witchcraft and evil deeds.

Religion in Sweden Today

Swedish children are members of the Lutheran Church of Sweden by birth. They continue to be members unless they withdraw formally. Nearly nine out of ten Swedes belong to the State Church today. While only a small minority of them attend church regularly, most participate in baptism, confirmation, marriage, and funeral ceremonies within the church.

Other faiths have been represented in small numbers since the end of the nineteenth century. These include a few other Protestant sects, as well as Roman Catholics, Orthodox, Jewish, Buddhist, and Muslim groups.

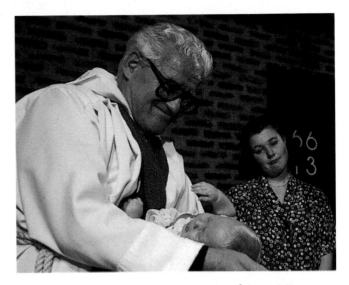

Most Swedes participate in Christian customs, such as baptism.

The Bridal Crown

Modern Swedish couples may be married in the church or at the courthouse. Most choose the church.

It is traditional at formal and semiformal weddings in many countries for the bride to wear a veil, sometimes topped with a simple crown of flowers. In Sweden, the bridal crown is a very important part of the tradition, even at very simple weddings.

In earlier times, people would be critical of a bride who did not wear a crown. Originally the crown was a simple headband wrapped in ribbons that streamed down the back. Then, for many generations, the custom was to wear a crown of myrtle leaves. Swedish descendants

living in foreign countries have been known to have authentic myrtle crowns made in Sweden and shipped to them.

The groom cuts an elegant figure, too, clad in full dress of white tie and tails.

Today, the bridal crown is usually made of silver and gold and sometimes set with precious stones. The Nordiska Museum, in Stockholm, has a collection of crowns, bridal gowns, and peasant costumes on display.

In Dalarna, brides often wear the colorful and traditional costume of their community (left). Bridal gowns in other parts of Sweden are white.

CHAPTER
NINE

The Fuller Life:
Arts and Sports

Country people of Sweden have an active folk culture with deep roots in their history. Local artists
perform, musicians play for dances, singers sing folk
ballads, and artisans create traditional handicrafts.

MORE FORMAL AND CLASSICAL CULTURAL ACTIVITIES HAVE been encouraged by kings and governments. King Gustav III established the Royal Opera House and the Royal Dramatic Theater in Stockholm in the late eighteenth century. But access to the performing arts, museums, and other cultural activities is sometimes difficult for people in remote regions.

Many wear traditional dress for Midsummer festivities.

The Swedish government makes contributions and subsidies to encourage theater, dance, music, literature, visual arts, museums, public libraries, and cultural magazines.

Music, Dance, Theater

Sweden's major cities have fine facilities and personnel for the performing arts. In addition, national touring companies put on top-level performances in many parts of the country. Regional theatrical and musical groups are also active. Outdoor summer concerts can be found all over Sweden, most of them free. Music festivals lasting for several days are held at thirty-five locations throughout the country.

Swedish performers do not earn the fabulous salaries earned by stars in some other countries. However, they do not have to undergo periods of unemployment either. They are paid yearly salaries and receive employee benefits and paid vacations, just

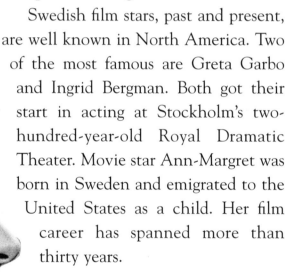

Above: **Greta Garbo**
Right: **Ann-Margret**
Below: **Ingrid Bergman**

as other professionals do. Acting is taught in theater academies in Stockholm, Göteborg, and Malmö.

In 1992, the Royal Dramatic Theater started the Theater for Young People. Plays of interest to children of all ages are performed as a part of the regular theater schedule.

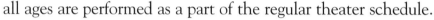

Swedish film stars, past and present, are well known in North America. Two of the most famous are Greta Garbo and Ingrid Bergman. Both got their start in acting at Stockholm's two-hundred-year-old Royal Dramatic Theater. Movie star Ann-Margret was born in Sweden and emigrated to the United States as a child. Her film career has spanned more than thirty years.

Ingmar Bergman is an internationally acclaimed Swedish filmmaker and theatrical producer. The Directors Guild of America honored him with their highest award in 1990. His sensitive films about human emotions have made him known as "the poet of joy and pain."

Much of Sweden's heritage is preserved in a wide variety of museums. Several of them are in the homes of famous artists. Alster Manor is near the town of Karlstad, on the north shore of Lake Vänern. It was the birthplace of one of Sweden's greatest poets, Gustav Fröding. Displays also tell about the history and industry of the region.

Not far away are two landmarks related to the author Selma Lagerlöf. One is Rottneros Manor, known to her readers as the setting for one of her novels. A fine sculpture park and garden surround the house, and a small children's zoo is on the grounds. The other is Mårbacka, Lagerlöf's home. In 1909, she became the first woman to receive the Nobel prize for literature. The house has been preserved exactly as it was when she died. Both of these homes are near the town of Sunne.

Selma Lageröf

Övralid, at Motala on the Göta Canal, is the beautiful home of the Swedish poet Verner von Heidenstam.

Carl Larsson was a much-loved Swedish painter who created idyllic illustrations of Swedish domestic life at the turn of the century. His cottage, Carl Larsson-Gården, attracts thousands of visitors each year to the little town of Sundborn, in Dalarna. His work was influenced by the local folk art. He dec-

Carl Larsson

Carl Milles's statue of Poseidon in Göteborg

orated just about everything in the cottage, including the doors, which he painted with family portraits.

Sundborn is near the historic mining town of Falun. The Dalarna Museum, in Falun, has an impressive collection of local folk paintings and other historic items. Selma Lagerlöf's one-time writing room has been reconstructed in the museum.

Zornsgården, the home and studio of painter Anders Zorn, who was a close friend of Carl Larsson, are preserved in the town of Mora, on Lake Siljan. There is also a museum of his work in Mora.

Waldemarsudde was the home of Prince Eugen, brother of King Gustav V. The prince was a landscape painter, and his home was willed to the nation. It is a lovely house and a fine gallery of paintings by the prince, and by other artists as well.

Swedish sculptor Carl Milles is famous for his beautiful fountains and lifelike figures that seem to be in motion. He worked in Sweden until he was in his fifties, then accepted a teaching position in the United States. He was commissioned to produce a number of public works for U.S. cities.

Milles kept a summer home in an island suburb of Stockholm. While there each year, he worked to create a sculpture garden that includes reproductions of statues on display in the United States. The statues of Millesgården are arranged on terraced cliffs overlooking the harbor.

Living History

There are dozens of castles scattered over the countryside of Skåne. Seven palaces, built over the past four centuries, are in the Stockholm area. Pictures of warriors in battle, ships, and people on hunting and fishing expeditions are carved on countless rocks in the region north and northeast of Göteborg. They were probably created during the Bronze Age, and they are Europe's largest collection of rock carvings.

Also in the Göteborg area is a thirteenth-century stave (wooden) church.

Everywhere in Sweden are reminders of what a long history this country has. And few countries have done a better job of preserving the artistic and historic culture of the people. Nearly every community has a small collection of preserved struc-

One of Sweden's many castles gracing the countryside

Småland is known for its glassworks.

Skansen, the world's largest open-air museum

tures that tell the story of that region's past. During at least part of the year, one finds costumed guides and artisans at work in these open-air museums, bringing history to life.

Mining history comes alive in communities of central and northern Sweden. The art of blowing and etching elegant glass works, for which this country is world-famous, is demonstrated in the Crystal Kingdom of Småland. Forestry museums commemorate the industry that has been the very foundation of the Swedish economy. Maritime museums celebrate the nation's shipbuilding prowess. The Ship Museum in Göteborg has twenty historic vessels on display.

Skansen is Sweden's largest and the world's oldest open-air museum. A sort of Sweden in miniature, it opened on the island of Djurgården, Stockholm, in 1891. It has about 150 houses and shops that typify different regions and periods of

Swedish heritage. Cobblers fashion hand-made shoes; potters and glassblowers create works of art; bakers and candy makers fill the air with the sweet scents of their products.

Djurgården is Stockholm's most popular gathering spot in summer. Major festivals, concerts, and dances offer modern entertainment with a living history background.

More Stockholm Museums

There are more than fifty museums in Stockholm. Two of the most important to Swedish culture in general are the National Maritime Museum and the Museum of National Antiquities.

A warship, Vasa, is a spectacular part of the Maritime Museum. Built in the 1620s, the ship sunk on her maiden voyage. The work of restoring the vessel has been going on since it was brought to the surface in 1961. Marine archaeologists have been putting a giant jigsaw puzzle together from fragments of the ship. Divers brought up more than 24,000 objects that show a slice of maritime life in the seventeenth century.

Vasa, a warship on exhibit at the National Maritime Museum in Stockholm

Stockholm's City Hall

Stockholm's most famous landmark is not a castle or a historic building. It is the Stadshuset, a massive twentieth-century structure that serves as city hall. It sits on the edge of Lake Mälaren and its 347-foot (105-m) square tower can be seen from all over the southern part of the city.

At the top of the tower, gleaming in the sun, are three golden crowns, the symbol of Sweden. Below them is an observation platform, built in the shape of an old harbor light. In summer, visitors can climb the stairs or take an elevator to the platform. The views in every direction are magnificent. A carillon on the tower plays historic martial music at scheduled times. Smaller towers, domes, and minarets rise from the light green copper roofs.

Tour guides tell their audiences about the many priceless paintings, tapestries, and other works of art. People stroll through flower-filled gardens.

Receptions for important guests are held in the Stadshuset. Visiting monarchs and presidents often arrive by water, in ceremonial boats. And, once a year, people from many parts of the world are invited here to attend Sweden's most important social and newsworthy event.

They assemble in the Golden Hall, one of the world's most spectacular rooms. Nineteen million gilded tiles cover the walls. The marble floor gleams and sparkles with reflected light. Banquet tables are set with the finest china, silver, and crystal.

But on this night, it is not the beauty of the room that has everyone thrilled and excited. It is the annual ceremony awarding the year's Nobel prizes (below), except for the prize for peace. That one—perhaps the most prestigious of all—is awarded at a similar ceremony on the same day in Oslo, Norway's capital.

The Museum of National Antiquities inaugurated a new permanent exhibit in the fall of 1994. The Gold Room, 23 feet (7 m) below ground level, contains priceless pieces of jewelry and religious objects from both ancient times and the Middle Ages. There are Bronze Age bowls made of thin gold foil, medallions embossed with figures of Norse gods and mythical characters, and treasures of both gold and silver created during the Viking period.

Literature

Storytelling and folk singing—which is usually a form of storytelling set to music—have a tradition in Scandinavian countries that goes back to the beginning of history. Rune stones, rock carvings in an ancient alphabet, are found in many parts of Sweden and other Nordic regions. Actual written works, mostly of a religious nature, came into use during the Middle Ages.

August Strindberg (painting by Richard Bergh)

August Strindberg is generally thought of as the father of Swedish drama and fiction. He wrote more than sixty plays, as well as numerous novels, essays, and short stories. His plays, in particular, gave him an international reputation. His career lasted more than forty years in the late 1800s and early 1900s.

Several Swedish writers have won the Nobel prize for literature. Selma Lagerlöf, who received the honor in 1909, wrote novels about Swedish farm life. Verner von Heidenstam won in 1916 and Eric Axel Karlfeldt in 1931, both for poetry. Pär Lagerkvist was honored in 1951 for his novels. Two Swedish writers shared the prize in 1974: novelist Eyvind

Johnson and Harry Martinson, for his work in several literary fields.

There are more than two thousand libraries in Sweden. About 120 book buses bring library selections to remote places. Children's libraries have existed in Sweden for about two hundred years.

Libraries present storytelling programs, puppet theater performances, interviews with authors, and other special events for children.

Arts and Crafts

In earlier times, Swedish people, like those in the rest of the world, could not go to the corner store or shopping center for things they used every day. The women spun, wove, and sewed the family's clothing, sheets and coverlets, curtains and

Astrid Lindgren

Astrid Lindgren is Sweden's most beloved writer of books for children. Her stories of Pippi Longstocking—a strong young girl who "could lift a whole horse if she wanted to"—have been translated into fifty languages. Children around the world have been enjoying them for more than fifty years.

Lindgren's stories are based on her own happy childhood on a Swedish farm. While growing up she made up fairy tales based on the nature she knew. She read everything she could get her hands on, including books about children in other countries. Two of her favorites were *Pollyanna* and *Anne of Green Gables*.

Everyone around Astrid Lindgren predicted she would become a writer when she grew up. A stubborn streak in her made her promise herself she never would be. But her two children loved the stories she made up, so after a while she started writing them down. She began winning prizes for her books as soon as they were published. Over the years, Astrid Lindgren has won dozens of awards and medals.

"When I write, I lie in bed and put the book down in shorthand, and I have the feeling that nothing outside exists—I'm just on my bed in my little room, and I can go and meet the people I want to."

draperies, and rugs. The men made furniture and tools out of wood and metal. Some of the men were rug makers, too.

These craftspeople were not satisfied with creating things that worked; they wanted them to be attractive—even beautiful—as well. Handicrafts became something to be proud of. The textiles were well designed and brightly colored; wooden objects were beautifully carved.

Superb design and craftsmanship are Swedish traditions that have survived in the industrial age. Swedish products, from cutlery to automobiles, have an international reputation for excellence.

Dalarna, in central Sweden, is known as the Folklore District. It is a popular destination for tourists, who come to enjoy folk festivals and folk crafts. Shops are full of brightly painted wooden chairs, chests, tabletops, and smaller objects.

An example of Dala painting

The Dalecarlian horse is a favorite souvenir.

Dala painting is a distinctive style of decoration that uses designs of floral objects and other motifs.

The Dalecarlian toy horse is a popular souvenir. This short, stocky, carved wooden figure is painted bright red with blue, yellow, and white decorations. This horse has long been regarded by international travelers as the symbol of Sweden.

Some handmade objects are described more accurately as fine art, rather than handicraft. One outstanding Swedish example is glass.

Småland is sometimes called the Crystal Kingdom because of the many glassworks located there. This region, too, benefits from tourism based on their industry. Travelers can visit several of the glass factories and watch the artists at work.

World-famous Orrefors crystal

The oldest company, Kosta, was founded in 1742. This firm turns out crystal, which is glass with a high lead content.

Orrefors, in business since 1898, is known around the world for art glass. Skilled glassblowers fashion the stemware, vases, bowls, and other pieces, then artists etch designs by hand on each finished piece. Orrefors stemmed glasses are used at the annual Nobel prize-awarding dinner in Stockholm.

Sports

Swedish people love the outdoors, and almost everyone participates in some kind of sport. At least half the population belongs to at least one of the thousands of community sports associations and company sports clubs all over the country. Noncommercial sports, open to everyone, are emphasized.

The nation has been represented in Olympic Games since the first modern ones in 1896. Since then, Sweden has won more than five hundred Olympic medals, including more than two hundred golds. In 1995, Swedish teams and individuals won twenty-two World Athletic Championship titles, in a great variety of sports. Some of their titles were in archery, canoeing, figure skating, swimming, and weight lifting.

Sweden's oldest sport is skiing. In early days, however, it was not thought of as a sport but as a means of transportation. It made it possible for people to travel over the deep snows of the northland. Ancient skis were very different from the ones used today. They were around 9 feet (3 m) long and 6 inches (15 cm) wide. Swedish ski troops were used in battle as early as 1200. Recreational skiing is probably less than two hundred years old. There are down-

Agneta Andersson (left) and Susanne Gunnarsson won gold medals for Sweden in kayaking at the 1996 Olympic Games.

Skiing is Sweden's oldest sport.

hill slopes and ski jumps in many Swedish communities. Thousands of people join in cross-country ski races.

Swedish children are encouraged to take part in all kinds of sports. Families go hiking and camping together in the forests and mountains. Hundreds of miles of trails in the mountains are marked with cairns (piles of rocks). Youth hostels are found all over the countryside. They are open to the public and are very inexpensive. Campers are expected to leave their campsites clean and to gather wood to replace any they have used. Children are taught orienteering—the skills needed to find their way in a wilderness area.

Soccer is popular for Swedish boys and girls.

Long summer vacations are a time for families to enjoy the country's more than 90,000 lakes. No one in Sweden has to travel very far for water sports—swimming, canoeing, and sailing.

Most communities have public swimming pools, skating rinks, and playing fields. Children who show talent and interest for sports can get special training at upper-secondary sports schools. Girls are encouraged as much as boys to take part in sports. They play on soccer teams, ride horseback, and practice gymnastics. Soccer (Europeans call it football) is the nation's favorite team sport.

Tennis is popular, and Sweden has a distinguished record in tennis. Between 1976 and 1990, Sweden won the Davis Cup three times; Björn Borg was a five-time Wimbledon champion; Stefan Edberg won the Australian Open Championship twice and was Wimbledon champion twice; Mats Wilander won the U.S. Open champion once, French Open twice, and Australian Open three times.

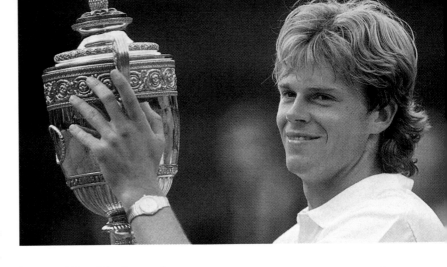

Stefan Edberg (above) and Björn Borg (below) are two of Sweden's best-known tennis players.

Golf courses are not as plentiful in Sweden as in some other countries. But there is one course in Lapland famous for playing at night. Here in summer, players can start their games at midnight and play in full sun until breakfast time.

Sweden has a motto, "Sport for all," including the physically handicapped. Special encouragement is given to children of new immigrants—they are taught the rules of games in their own languages.

Sport is considered an important part of good health care.

At Home, in School, on Holiday

Families in Sweden spend a great deal of time together. Even in one-parent families or when both parents are working, children and adults share many activities together.

When there is a young baby in the family, one of the parents is probably staying home to care for it. The government provides an allowance for this. The parent can take a leave of absence from work without losing the job. Preschool children of working parents go to day-care centers.

Families spend as much time together as they can.

School is very important in Sweden.

OLDER CHILDREN FIND A LOT OF THINGS TO DO AFTER school. They play group games, go to scout meetings, or spend time at a leisure-time center or library. Some of them are taking music or dancing lessons.

Horseback riding is a favorite hobby, especially with girls. Another is working with computers. A great many Swedish families have home computers and almost all of them have television.

Swedish children watch TV shows from several different countries. They see some of the same programs and movies, and they hear the same popular songs, as children do in the United States.

Schools

Swedish people have a great respect for education. All children between the ages of seven and sixteen are required to go to school. But education

Many students go on to universities.

doesn't stop there. Adults attend various kinds of classes, and they read a lot. They buy more newspapers and magazines than people in many other countries.

This love of learning is an old tradition in Sweden. The first university was established in 1477. Freedom of the press has existed since 1766. A law establishing compulsory education was passed by the parliament in 1842. Every parish (or town) was required to have a school and a teacher.

All schooling in Sweden is free, including books, paper, and hot lunches. For those who need it, free transportation and even free clothing are also available. A schoolchild's day in Sweden is much like that of pupils in North America.

Everyone is taught to read. Reading Swedish is easier to learn than reading English, because the language is relatively phonetic. That is, each letter is pronounced the same way in most every word, and there are only a few silent letters. So once youngsters know the Swedish alphabet, they can usually teach themselves to read with very little help.

Playtime

A lot of playtime is built into the school day in Sweden. There are frequent breaks between classes, and the children are usually expected to spend that time outdoors in the fresh air. This is part of the Swedish philosophy of using games and sports to keep fit and have good health.

Most of the games children play are similar to those enjoyed by children in North America. There are variations on such old favorites such as "Simon Says" and "Farmer in the Dell." One game played on a gym floor is something like field hockey.

Gummiband (rubber band) is a little like jump rope. Two children face each other with a giant rubber band between them, attached to their ankles. Other players perform tricks in between.

Several games using marbles are much more popular in Sweden than they are these days in most of North America.

Mathematics is a little easier, too, because they use the metric system. All measurements are based on units of ten. Distances are measured in kilometers instead of miles, weights in kilograms instead of pounds, and lengths in centimeters and meters instead of inches and feet.

By about the third grade, all pupils begin to learn a second language—English. They study it for at least three years. They are delighted to find quite a few words are either identical or very similar in Swedish and English. That is because both languages developed from Germanic languages. Most children also hear a lot of English on the radio and television and in movies. Special classes in Swedish are given for the children of immigrants.

Both boys and girls have classes in woodwork and metal work, and both learn child care and sewing.

Seventh graders begin to learn a third language. They talk with vocational counselors about what they may want to do

Family Vacation

Swedish school children look forward to several vacations each year. They have two weeks off for Christmas, a week in February, and a week for Easter. The summer vacation lasts from June to mid-August.

Most Swedish families try to spend at least part of the long vacation in a summer cabin. Many adults have long summer vacations, too. The summer homes are on one of the thousands of islands on the east or west coast or on lakeshores in southern and central Sweden.

The families spend as much time outdoors as possible. They swim, boat, and fish. They hike in the forests and pick mushrooms and wild strawberries, lingonberries,

raspberries, blueberries, and cloudberries. Sometimes they practice orienteering.

At the end of February, schools are closed for a week so families can enjoy a winter vacation, too. This is usually called the ski vacation. The trains are filled with children and adults heading for the mountains and for Lapland.

Occasionally a family may decide to spend the week in the south of Spain or some other warm and sunny place instead. But during winter evenings and weekends, they will probably head for slopes and cross-country trails near home.

when they grow up. They can start classes in fields that interest them, such as science or one of the arts. Of course, they can change their minds later on if they want to.

Eighth graders get a chance to learn about the occupations they may want to go into. They spend time as aides in hospitals, schools, or mechanical shops.

In ninth grade, the pupils are given a choice of three general areas—arts and social studies, science and technical studies, or economic and commercial studies. Many different programs are available, and all of them are open to both boys and girls.

Official Holidays in Sweden

New Year's Day	January 1
Epiphany	January 6
Labor Day	May 1
Midsummer Day	Saturday nearest June 24
All Saints' Day	November 5
Christmas	December 25–26

Movable religious holidays include:

Good Friday, Easter Monday, Ascension, and Whitmonday

Further Education

Teenagers who plan on a university education go to schools called gymnasiums, for the tenth, eleventh, and twelfth grades.

Graduation from the gymnasium is a time for great celebration. The student is given a white cap, a symbol of academic success. Families hold parties, shower gifts on the graduate, and drive through the streets in flower-trimmed cars and trucks.

About one-third of the graduates go on to university or professional college. Tuition is free in Sweden, and in some cases the government also pays a student's living expenses. Entrance to the university is highly competitive, however, because space is limited. So not everyone who wants to can be sure of attending a university.

Many graduates who go to work immediately do opt for further education after a few years. They may take correspondence or television courses or join study circles.

Folk schools are an old Scandinavian tradition. One of them, the Söranger Folk School, is more than a hundred years old. These are a type of boarding school, with courses lasting from twenty to thirty-four weeks during winter. Adults who did not attend high school can make up those courses in folk school. They can also take courses in handicraft and other hobbies.

Some Swedish companies run special schools to train workers in skills that will be useful on the job. Nearly one adult out of three in Sweden takes part in some form of adult education. School buildings are used for adult classes. Other school facilities, such as swimming pools, are open for public use after regular school hours.

Festivals and Holidays

The way people celebrate special holidays and festivals is always a mixture of old traditions and new customs. The Vikings, medieval Catholics, and German merchants all contributed rituals that survive in Swedish celebrations today. The practices evolved and merged over the centuries. In modern times, new customs are added that show the influences of recent immigrants and international television shows.

The New Year comes into Sweden much as it does in other parts of the world. People crowd into the streets on New Year's Eve, and promptly at midnight, bells ring, whistles blow, and fireworks explode.

Opposite: **Fireworks on New Year's Eve in Stockholm**

Good Friday, for many families, is a solemn religious observance, and they go to church on Easter Sunday. Children and adults get together to dye and decorate Easter eggs. Florists sell thousands of yellow daffodils to brighten family homes.

Walpurgis Night is April 30. This festival is of German origin and hails the coming of spring with big bonfires and lots of merrymaking. At Uppsala, for example, students throw their winter hats into the river, put on their white velvet graduation caps, and begin a twenty-four-hour period of cheering and singing.

A Midsummer festival

Midsummer is celebrated on the weekend closest to the summer solstice, in late June. It is a big celebration, with games, music, dances, parades, and feasts. A large pole is decorated with leaves and flowers—an adaptation of the Maypole used in other European countries. Even in southern Sweden, there is some light all night at this time of year. In earlier days, unmarried girls used to make a small bouquet of nine different kinds of flowers and place it under their pillows. This was supposed to make them dream of their future husbands. Today's young Swedish women believe in making up their own minds about such matters.

In August, when most school and work holidays are almost over, Swedes have an excuse for more parties. Crayfish—a smaller, freshwater version of the lobster—are in season and plentiful. People get together to enjoy music and fireworks and to eat their fill of fresh boiled crayfish.

Crayfish are plentiful in August.

Jansson's Frestelse

A dish often served to guests of Swedish families is called Jansson's *frestelse*, or Jansson's temptation. It is named, according to Swedish lore, for a religious man named Eric Jansson. He led a small group of immigrants to America in 1846, to form a religious commune. They traveled by boat through canals and lakes to Chicago, then walked 160 miles (265 km) to western Illinois. They named their community Bishop Hill, after Jansson's birthplace in Sweden.

Eric Jansson was a Pietist. He believed in a simple life of devotion and purity and rejected the dogma and ritual of the Lutheran Church. Among other things, Jansson preached against the "pleasures of the flesh," including overeating. On one occasion, he shocked his disciples when someone served him this casserole and he ate it all.

The recipe calls for six raw potatoes, peeled and cut into strips, ten or twelve fresh or canned anchovies cut in small pieces, and some chopped onions. These ingredients are layered in a baking dish with butter and breadcrumbs in between the layers. Two cups of rich cream are poured over the mixture, which is then baked in a 375°F oven until the potatoes are soft and there is a light-brown crust on top.

All Saints' Day, November 1, is a day for decorating the graves of fallen heroes and departed family members.

December 10 is not a holiday or festival day, but it is a very important date in Sweden—and to many people all over the world. This is the date for the annual presentation ceremony honoring Nobel prize winners.

Food

For everyday meals, Swedes like such dishes as hearty soups, salads, meatballs, stuffed cabbage leaves, roast meats, and fish prepared in many ways. Dessert may be fruit salad, rice pudding, or some kind of pastry. Pea soup and a dessert of pancakes is a traditional meal for Thursdays. Most restaurants and many homes follow this tradition. Cheeses are popular, and some Swedes eat fish nearly every day.

Birthdays are celebrated with coffee parties, and traditionally feature seven kinds of cakes and sweet breads. A wedding celebration calls for a huge *spettekaka*, a "spit cake." Dozens of eggs are beaten with sugar and a little flour, and the batter is dripped slowly onto a cone-shaped spit over a fire, to form lacy layers.

Holiday Eating

Just about every Swedish holiday has a specific food associated with it. *Fettisdagsbullar* is served for dessert on Shrove Tuesday and on every Tuesday during Lent. It is a large bun filled with almond paste, topped with whipped cream, and served in a bowl of warm milk.

Waffles are eaten on Lady Day (the Sunday nearest March 25), halibut on Good Friday, and hard-boiled eggs on Easter Eve. Easter dinner's main dish is often lamb.

At one time, Swedes celebrated their hero, King Gustav II Adolph, on November 6, the day he was killed in battle in 1632. The day is no longer observed with any formal celebrations, but it is traditional to eat Gustav Adolph pastry with afternoon coffee that day. The pastry is made in the shape of the king's head or decorated with his portrait.

Roast goose, stuffed with apples and prunes, has been the traditional main dish of St. Martin's Day, November 11, a Catholic holy day. Swedish Protestants continue the custom, but eat "St. Martin's goose" the day before, which is Martin Luther's birthday.

Fettisdagsbullar, **baked prior to Lent**

Special buns, called "Lucia cats," are served on St. Lucia's Day.

Many special dishes, breads, and cookies are prepared for Christmas. *Lutfisk* is dried codfish, soaked, boiled, and served with a thick cream gravy. A huge ham is prepared in several ways. For dessert there will usually be *ostkaka*, a rich almond-flavored custard served with fruit or jam.

A few hours before it is time to start preparing the main Christmas feast, a simple soup of meat and vegetables is put on the stove to simmer. Since the

A festive Christmas table

cooks of the family are all very busy getting ready for the feast, other people in the household get their own lunch. They find a bowl, spoon, and piece of bread, and help themselves to *dopp i grytan*, a dip in the kettle.

The Smörgåsbord

The Swedish word *smörgåsbord* has found its way into many other languages. *Smör* means butter, or spread, and *smörgås* has come to stand for bread that has been spread with something—an open-faced sandwich. *Bord* means table, or board, as in room and board.

So literally, a smörgåsbord means a table loaded with sandwiches. But it has come to mean much more. Around the world, the word smorgasbord (as it is spelled in English), brings visions of a large display of all kinds of foods set out on long tables. It means "help yourself" and "all you can eat."

All in all, a typical Swedish smörgåsbord has literally dozens and dozens of different dishes. A smörgåsbord is used for special occasions and can be found in most hotels and restaurants in the country.

Here are some of the usual foods. Fish dishes are grouped together—pickled herring, herring in cream, salmon with

Opposite: **A Swedish smörgåsbord**

dill, marinated salmon, and oysters with mustard sauce. The cold dishes come next—a variety of cheeses, cottage cheese, a raw vegetable tray, pickled beets, and salads of fresh fruits. In the hot section, choices include stuffed pork loin, meatballs, sliced ham and turkey, rice and potatoes fixed several ways, brown beans, and vegetable casseroles. Several kinds of bread, plus butter, are offered. Sometimes the butter is a pyramid of tiny balls; sometimes it has been carved into miniature birds.

Then for those who have any appetite left, there is the dessert table with cookies, fruit bread, rice pudding, custard, cheesecake, and fruit tarts.

Sweden's way of life stands for much that is good—for sharing, for excellence in workmanship, for international cooperation, and for the promotion of peace.

And as a symbol of hospitality and celebration, nothing can surpass the Swedish smörgåsbord!

Timeline

c. 2500 B.C. Egyptians build the Pyramids and Sphinx in Giza.

563 B.C. Buddha is born in India.

A.D. 313 The Roman emperor Constantine recognizes Christianity.

610 The prophet Muhammad begins preaching a new religion called Islam.

Swedish History

862 Rurik, a Swede, founds the Russian city of Novgorod

875–900 Saint Ansgar tries to introduce Christianity to the Swedes

1054 The Eastern (Orthodox) and Western (Roman) Churches break apart.

1066 William the Conqueror defeats the English in the Battle of Hastings.

1095 Pope Urban II proclaims the First Crusade.

1160 Swedish King Eric IX is assassinated by a disgruntled Danish prince

1215 King John seals the Magna Carta.

1300s The Renaissance begins in Italy.

1319 Sweden and Norway are united by Magnus VII

1347 The Black Death sweeps through Europe.

1362 Finland becomes a Swedish province

1397 Union of Kalmar unites Danes, Finns, Norwegians, and Swedes under one crown

1435 Arboga assembly established, first Riksdag (parliament) in Swedish history

1453 Ottoman Turks capture Constantinople, conquering the Byzantine Empire.

1477 University of Uppsala founded

1492 Columbus arrives in North America.

1500s The Reformation leads to the birth of Protestantism.

1520 Christian II, king of Denmark, massacres Swedish nobles, an incident which is later known as the Stockholm Bloodbath

1523 Gustav Vasa becomes the first hereditary Swedish monarch

1556 Finland made a grand duchy of Sweden

Swedish History		World History	
Thirty Years' War	1618–1648		
Gustavus Adolphus killed at the Battle of Lutzen	1632		
Karl XII becomes king	1697		
Swedes are defeated by Russians	1709		
Sweden's "Age of Freedom"	1718–1773		
War between Russia and Sweden, resulting in cession of part of Finland to Russia	1741–1743		
		1776	The Declaration of Independence is signed.
War between Sweden and Russia	1788–1790	1789	The French Revolution begins.
First Swedish constitution adopted; Norway becomes a Swedish territory	1809		
Riksdag introduces compulsory education	1842	1865	The American Civil War ends.
Norway becomes independent of Sweden	1905		
World War I; Sweden remains neutral	1914–1918	1914	World War I breaks out.
Sweden adopts parliamentary government	1917	1917	The Bolshevik Revolution brings Communism to Russia.
Introduction of universal suffrage (all citizens over eighteen can vote)	1921	1929	Worldwide economic depression begins.
World War II; Sweden remains neutral but aides refugees escaping from Germany and Nazi-held territory	1939–1945	1939	World War II begins, following the German invasion of Poland.
		1957	The Vietnam War starts.
Riksdag becomes a one-house assembly	1971		
Carl XVI Gustav becomes king	1973		
Constitution revised	1974		
Social Democrats defeated after forty-four years in power; the Center party and other non-Socialists form government	1976		
Act of Succession	1980		
Social Democrats are returned to power	1982		
Assassination of Prime Minister Olof Palme	1986		
		1989	The Berlin Wall is torn down, as Communism crumbles in Eastern Europe.
		1996	Bill Clinton re-elected U.S. president.

Fast Facts

Official name: Kingdom of Sweden

Stockholm

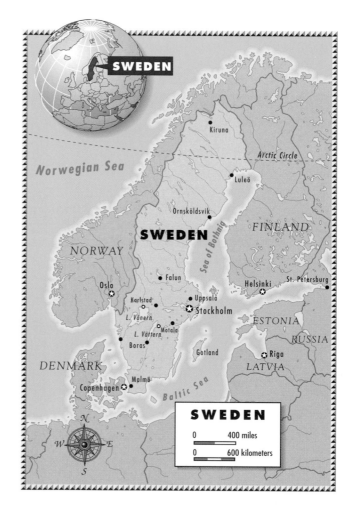

Capital: Stockholm

Official language: Swedish

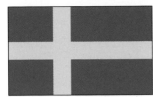

Flag of Sweden

King Carl and Queen Sylvia

Official religion:	Church of Sweden (Lutheran)
National anthem:	"Du gamla, du fria, du fjallhoga nord" (O Glorious Old Mountain, Crowned Land of the North)
Chief of state:	King
Head of government:	Prime minister
Area and dimensions:	The country covers 173,732 square miles (449,964 sq km) of which 15,071 square miles (39,035 sq km) is made up of inland bodies of water. Sweden stretches about 980 miles (1,575 km) from north to south and about 310 miles (500 km) from east to west. It has a coastline of 4,700 miles (7,600 km).
Bordering countries:	Norway to the West, Finland to the East
Average temperature:	Stockholm - February, 26°F (−3°C) - July, 64°F (18°C)
Location:	55 degrees 20′ to 69 degrees 4′ North; 10 degrees 58′ to 24 degrees 10′ East
Average annual rainfall:	24 inches (61 cm)
Largest lake:	Vänern, covering 2,156 square miles (5,584 sq km)
Territorial sea limit:	12 miles
Highest elevation:	Mt. Kebnekaise, 6,926 feet (2,111 m)
Lowest elevation:	Sea level along the coasts
National population: (1995 est.)	8,816,381

The Royal Palace

Population of largest cities in Sweden:		
	Stockholm	684,576
	Göteborg	444,553
	Malmö	242,706
	Uppsala	181,191
	Linköping	130,489

Famous landmarks: Royal Palace (Stockholm); the "garden city" of Göteborg, the resort island of Götland off the Baltic coast; and the lake and mountain country in the north. Cultural centers in Stockholm include the Royal Opera, the Royal Dramatic Theater, and the Berwald Concert Hall.

Industry: Since the 1930s, industrial development has boomed in Sweden and quickly replaced agriculture as a primary economic force. Today, Sweden's industry is highly developed and exports include automobiles, planes, and ships.

Currency: The krona is a paper currency of 100 öre. There are coins of 50 öre and 1, 2, 5, and 10 kronor, and notes of 5, 10, 20, 50, 100, 500, and 1,000 kronor. In 1999, U.S.$1 = 8.34kr.

Weights and measures:	Metric system
Literacy:	Virtually 100%

Common Swedish words and phrases:	*helmslöjd*	traditional handcrafted Swedish products made in people's homes
	klappa	clap, tap, pat, or pet
	loppet	a ski race
	middag	the midday meal, usually eaten in the late afternoon
	ombudsman	an official who looks into complaints about the government made by citizens
	runes	an ancient script that was carved on stones and written on sheepskin
	skalds	ancient singers who celebrated heroic deeds and great events
	smörgåsbord	a table loaded with a variety of foods, like a buffet
	ja	yes

To Find Out More

Nonfiction

▶ Cohat, Yves. *The Vikings: Lords of the Sea.* New York: Harry N. Abrams, Inc., Publishers, 1992.

▶ Gould, Dennis E., *Let's Visit Sweden.* Bridgeport, CT: Burke Publishing Company, 1984.

▶ Knowlton, MaryLee, and Mark J. Sachner, eds. *Children of the World, Sweden.* Milwaukee: Gareth Stevens Publishing, 1987.

▶ McGill, Allyson. *The Swedish Americans.* New York: Chelsea House Publishers, 1988.

▶ Nicholson, Robert, and Claire Watts. *The Vikings.* New York: Chelsea Juniors, 1994.

▶ Odijk, Pamela. *The Vikings.* Englewood Cliffs, NJ: Silver Burdett Press, 1989.

▶ Olsson, Kari. *Sweden: A Good Life for All.* Minneapolis: Dillon Press, 1983.

▶ Thompson, Martha Wiberg, ed. *Superbly Swedish.* Iowa City: Penfield Press, 1983.

▶ Visual Geography Series. *Sweden in Pictures.* Minneapolis: Lerner Publications, 1990.

Fiction

▶ Lindgren, Astrid. *Pippi Longstocking.* New York: Viking Press, 1950.

Folklore

▶ Blecher, Lone Thygesen, and George Blecher. *Swedish Folktales and Legends.* New York: Pantheon Books, 1993.

Reference

▶ *Berlitz Pocket Guide to Sweden.* New York: Berlitz, 1994.

▶ *Berlitz Swedish Phrase Book.* New York: Berlitz, 1989

▶ Brown, Jules, and Mick Sinclair. *The Real Guide, Scandinavia.* New York: Prentice Hall, 1990.

▶ Fullerton, Brian, and Alan F. Williams. *Scandinavia, an Introductory Geography.* New York: Prager Publishers, 1972.

▶ Mead, W.R., and Wendy Hall. *Scandinavia.* New York: Walker and Company, 1972.

▶ Moberg, Vilhelm. A *History of the Swedish People from Prehistory to the Renaissance.* New York: Pantheon Books, 1972.

▶ Morris, Ingrid. *Visitor's Guide, Sweden.* New York: Hunter Publishing, 1994.

▶ Nordstrom, Byron J., ed. *Dictionary of Scandinavian History.* Greenwood Press, 1986.

▶ Taylor, Doreen, ed. *Insight Guides, Sweden.* New York: APA Publications, Ltd., 1995.

Videotapes

▶ Lark, Ed. *The Spirit of Sweden.* Englewood, CO: Quantum Communications, 1989.

▶ *Scandinavia* is a ten-part television series originally broadcast on PBS. These tapes can be ordered from South Carolina TV.

Websites

▶ **The Royal Court of Sweden**
http://www.royalcourt.se/eng/index.
html
*Detailed information on the monarchy,
the royal family, and the royal palaces*

▶ **The Swedish Information
Smorgasbord**
http://www.sverigeturism.se/
smorgasbord/
*A broad overview of culture, industry,
nature, society, sports, and trade*

▶ **The Swedish Page**
http://www.svenska-sidor.com/
*A wide variety of links includes Virtual
Sweden and information about the
Nobel prize, schools, government agen-
cies, municipalities, and libraries.*

▶ **Young Sweden**
http://www.si.se/young/index.htm
*A page devoted to Swedish youth on the
Swedish Institute site. Includes interviews with several Swedish teenagers:
where some teenagers work, how they
spend their leisure time, and what their
values are.*

Organizations and Embassies

▶ **American Swedish Institute**
2600 Park Avenue
Minneapolis, MN 55407
(612) 871-4907

▶ **Scandinavian Tourism Bureau**
655 Third Avenue
New York, NY 10017
(212) 949-2333

▶ **Swedish Consulate General**
885 Second Avenue
New York, NY 10017
(212) 583-2550

▶ **Swedish Embassy**
600 New Hampshire Avenue, NW
Washington, DC 20037
(202) 944-5600

Index

Page numbers in *italics* indicate illustrations

About the Author

Sylvia McNair was born in Korea and believes she inherited a love of travel from her missionary parents. She grew up in Vermont. After graduating from Oberlin College, she held a variety of jobs, married, had four children, and settled in the Chicago area. She now lives in Evanston, Illinois. She is the author of several travel guides and a dozen books for young people published by Children's Press.

"The first step to writing a book is to read. I always head for the library, sometimes several different libraries. When writing about a country, I start with encyclopedias and other reference books. I send for any materials published by the U.S. government about the country I'm studying. Often I go to bookstores and pick up a guidebook or two. Sometimes I buy a phrase book or dictionary of the country's language. I use my computer to search for information on the Internet.

"Next I make contact, in person if possible, with the nation's tourist office, embassy, and consulate. I ask a lot of questions. I gratefully accept all the printed material any of these officials are willing to give me.

"If I can find any people from that nation living in my area, I arrange to interview them. Graduate students who are studying in this country are always a great source, and fun to get to know, as well. I've made some lasting friendships that way. If I have a chance to visit the country I'm writing about, I pack my bags.

"Last (although I've been working on it all along) comes the writing part. I sit at my computer for several hours each day. I use up reams of paper as I print out many drafts before I'm satisfied with the result.

"And while I'm writing, I'm imagining that I am visiting that country, maybe even that I'm living there. Writing about places is almost as good an adventure as traveling to them."

McNair has traveled on all the continents except Antarctica. "Every region has its own unique charm," she says. "And the more I learn about the Scandinavian countries, the more I admire them."

Photo Credits

Photographs ©: